Straw -
May unconditi
and compassion always
touch your life.

With warmest wishes -
Pamela Wilson

Thank you for providing
a caring home to special
furry loves who have
touched our lives -
and for having a kind
heart for all creatures
great and small.
With love and warmest
wishes always -

www.Tubblewoodtales.com
www.amazon.com

PUPPY PAL POINTERS:

FROM THE TRUE TAILS OF RIPPLE AND JESSIE

As shared with Pamela J. Wilson

Tips for dogs of all ages

authorHOUSE™

1663 LIBERTY DRIVE, SUITE 200
BLOOMINGTON, INDIANA 47403
(800) 839-8640
WWW.AUTHORHOUSE.COM

First published by AuthorHouse 03/23/05

ISBN: 1-4208-0628-9 (sc)
ISBN: 1-4208-0629-7 (hc)

Printed in the United States of America
Bloomington, Indiana

This book is printed on acid-free paper.

About the Book

Did you say "I love you" to your faithful pet today? If so, you are not alone; approximately 91% of pet owners have said those same words to their pets at least once. No doubt about it, animals play an integral part of the family unit and, in some cases, can be one of the most important beings in a person's life. With an estimated 60% of US households containing a companion animal, there are plenty of reasons to read *Puppy Pal Pointers: From the True Tails of Ripple and Jessie.*

Although technically puppies are young dogs, puppy pal pointers relate to dogs of all ages. The book consists of subjects pertinent to every devoted pet owner, including caring for, treating, understanding, treasuring, bonding with, and grieving for your dog, plus pet care tips for kids. Wide realms of topics pertaining to pet care and responsible ownership are covered, such as vaccinations, parasite control, hygiene, overpopulation concerns, relationships with cats, diet, the human-animal bond, aging, pet loss, and the grief process. What makes *Puppy Pal Pointers* different from other pet care books is that it is told through the insightful eyes of Ripple and Jessie Wilson. These two wise pups relay true stories of their lives and times and relate them to the everyday needs of dogs everywhere. Every short segment ends with a pointer created by their perceptive minds, plus favorite quotations and poetry are sprinkled throughout the text. As a treat to readers, their pictures, along with photos of their canine and feline peers, are used to accentuate concepts.

Ripple Wilson (RW) was born in Illinois and traveled to Texas at the tender age of two. He is lean and lanky with a short, tri-colored coat. His three-legged stature never affected his physical energy or his spiritual perfection. Jessie Wilson (JW), his non-blood sister, was born and raised in Texas. She has the grace and flawless beauty of a red fox. Her feisty, demanding personality is a contrast to Ripple's gentle, generous nature. Together they have weaved a blend for telling their own personal tales about each other and their friends.

Ripple and Jessie have spent their lives with the person who belongs to them, Pamela Wilson, RVT, MEd, CHES. She has had articles published in the *Journal of the American Veterinary Medical Association* and *Texas Veterinarian* and is the editor of the *Animal Control Officer Training Manual.* She was named Humane Educator for 2000 by the Texas Animal Control Association and Veterinary Technician of the Year for 2002 by the Texas Veterinary Medical Association; she also received the Alumni Achievement Award from Spoon River College. Although she is not a veterinarian (and, therefore, not attempting to diagnose or supply medical counsel), she worked at a small animal clinic for 14 years. She currently works with zoonoses at the state health department and is a recipient of the Honors for Excellence in Achievement, Leadership, and Teamwork in Health (H.E.A.L.T.H.) Award. Additionally, she teaches veterinary medical terminology at a community college, so she has been equipped to assist Ripple and Jessie with the phrasing of their remarks. She graduated with honors while earning a Bachelor of Science from Southern Illinois University and a Master of Education from the University of Texas, plus she is a Registered Veterinary Technician and a Certified Health Education Specialist. She has included sage teachings of a fictional critter named Miss Duck in her children's book, *Tales From Tubblewood: A Duck For All Seasons.*

Preface

"This book is intended to provide entertainment and make candid canine observations. It presents real-life situations to create awareness of potential health problems, not give medical advice. Scenarios portraying the human-animal bonding and grieving processes are also demonstrated. The reflection of love for special companions, who make such minor demands upon us, is at the heart of these writings. Friends come in two-legged, three-legged (not necessarily born that way), and four-legged versions. The person who helps share these stories with the reader loves all creatures great and small, in all states of health, and with all of her heart; I think it shows. Hopefully, you will find the information given worthwhile, and it will benefit some of your special companions."

Ernest "Skip" Oertli, DVM, PhD, Diplomate ACVPM

Dedicated to William D. and Mary A. Wilson,
who offered their compassion to all creatures

Special thanks to Dr. Skip Oertli,
Auntie Carol, Aaron, Straw,
and our grandma, Mary A. Wilson,
for their gracious review of our stories

Also thanks to our friends and extended family at
Hyde Park Animal Clinic
for their continuous love, caring, and support

Front cover photo featuring Ripple
by Mary Gottwald

Back cover photo featuring Jessie
by S. Caddel-Martin

Table of Contents

Introduction: Ripple's Roots

My name is Jessie Wilson, and I'm in my teens. With all those years behind me, my memory isn't what it used to be. If I'm going to share this story, I had better do it now. It's a story about the true life and times of my older brother, Ripple. It's a story of courage, adventure, and love. I think you will be the better for hearing about it. I know I am the better for having been part of it.

Not much is known about my brother when he was a young pup. His first nine months remain a bit of a mystery. He never talked about that time in his life. I guess he didn't believe in living in the past when the present was so good. We do know that he lived for a while with a family who had lots of kids. Chances are they were pretty good to him, too, as he always liked little folks. He also was known by another name then: Snoopy. He was mostly white with black patches (accentuated by touches of brown on his face). Go figure where his first owners got that original name!

Story has it that one fine spring day, Ripple was hit by a car. Not knowing what to do, he hightailed it under his house. His owners tried to coax him out, but it hurt him too much to move. After a few days, they were finally able to get him to Dr. Larry. Unfortunately for Ripple, those few days would cost him dearly. His long, thin, right hind leg had been broken by the car. While he was under the house, it had become badly infected. By the time Dr. Larry saw him, gangrene had taken over the leg. The only cure was to amputate it.

Dr. Larry was a country veterinarian who spent more time with horses and cattle than with dogs and cats. He told Ripple's (aka Snoopy's) owners that, because he was such a young dog, they should euthanize him and start over with a new puppy. It would be much cheaper for them in the long run. It's not that Dr. Larry didn't have a good heart. He was just used to working for folks who were, in general, more concerned about costs than the human-animal bond when treating an animal. It was a good thing for Ripple that his owners cared enough about him to beg Dr. Larry to save his life. The bad thing was, after all was said and done, they didn't care enough about him to pay his doctor bill. That's the point in his story where our mama entered.

Mama had grown up in Ripple's hometown. It was a small farming community in Central Illinois. When Ripple had his accident, she was away at college. Fate later brought them together. You see, Mama was crazy about animals, especially dogs. When she came home from college in May for the summer, she got a job working for Dr. Larry. She often told us about her first day there. While she was cleaning the kennel room, she opened a chain-link door to move a dog from one run to another. The dog slid on the slick cement floor to a sitting position and stared at her with big brown eyes. She then noticed that the part of his right leg below the stifle joint (knee) was gone. She looked at his record. It was marked "GMC" (Dr. Larry's short form for "General Motors Syndrome," which meant he had been hit by a car). She looked at the dog again. No doubt about it, it was puppy love at first sight.

Ripple had been in the hospital for a month before Mama started working there. His owners had not been to visit him, and Dr. Larry was pretty sure that he had seen the last of them. Mama felt sorry for any dog being in an enclosed run that long, so she used to let Ripple roam the animal clinic when Dr. Larry was away on a farm call and his other conscientious assistants, Louise and Pat, had left for the day. It was good for Ripple and for Mama because they kept each other company. They also were getting attached to each other, and Mama knew that this could be bad news. In August, she would have to go back to college. The place where she lived did not want dogs and would charge her $50.00 more per month if she had one (that was a lot of money in those days, especially for a student). With that in mind, Mama and Dr. Larry made it their mission to find Ripple a home. They showed him to almost every client who entered the clinic. Although some were impressed with his smiling face and whirling tail, there were no offers of a home. After so many rejections, Dr. Larry started to suggest that maybe Ripple should be euthanized.

Mama was so worried about Ripple's fate that her parents began to worry about her. They offered to take a look at Ripple themselves, although they already had a family dog and really didn't want another one. Ripple liked them immediately and turned on the charm so much that they said Mama could bring him to their home.

Before Ripple could go home, he had to have more surgery. Usually when a dog has a hind leg amputated, the veterinarian removes it at the hip joint no matter where the break is. This is because dogs tend to keep trying to use the stub of leg that's left; this would cause it to become raw and infected on the end. Dr. Larry, who was young and always trying new things, decided to experiment with Ripple; he removed only the infected part of Ripple's leg. However, a sharp piece of bone was still rubbing the tip of the stub and making it bleed. Dr. Larry wanted to operate and smooth the bone before Ripple left the clinic. At the same time, he decided to neuter Ripple. He said Ripple would get along better with other dogs that way. After all of this, Ripple was finally able to go home.

July 4, 1978, was a day to go down in infamy. Mama's big brother, our Uncle Jeff, drove her to the clinic to pick up my big brother. The clinic was closed that day, so Mama thought it would be a good time for her to spend getting Ripple used to his new home. As Ripple curled up on the front seat of the car for his departure from the animal clinic, his new uncle said, "Welcome home, Ripple." The two of them became fast friends. Ripple was close to a year of age on the day that he went to his new home. July 4th was truly Independence Day for him, so it now marked his official birthday. It was a day that would be celebrated in his honor every year from that day forward. By the way, Mama named him after the Grateful Dead song (which she thought should become the national anthem after Ripple became an integral part of her life), not the cheap wine!

Mama decided to take Ripple with her to college and pay the extra money for rent. She just couldn't leave Ripple behind, plus his puppy energy was a bit much for his grandparents to handle. She had learned from her parents that your dog depended on you, so you always put his needs first. That could mean living on cans of soup or boxes of macaroni and cheese, but you did what you had to do to provide for him. The longer Mama had Ripple, the more she realized that paying higher rent in order to keep him was the best money she ever spent.

Mama always said that she would forever be thankful to Ripple's first owners. She didn't admire them for abandoning Ripple, but they did convince Dr. Larry to save his life. By doing so, they gave her one of the best beings that ever graced her life. Mine too!

Jessie Wilson (JW)

Introduction: Jessie's Journey

I guess you could say that I was the key in determining Jessie's fate. She didn't have a good start in life. The first name her original owners had put on her medical record was "Dumbsh--." Doesn't leave a dog with much to aspire to, does it? The second name they unimaginatively gave her was "Coyote," supposedly because of her extra-long, pointed ears. If anything, she looked almost identical to a red fox, especially when she curled up for a nap and placed her thick, bushy tail across her nose. It shows how little her former owners knew!

It was no surprise when, after yet another bad break (you can take that literally) in her life, they wanted her euthanized at the veterinary clinic following a hit-and-run car accident. It always amazed me that owners let their puppy pals run loose, but then they don't want to foot the bill when the poor animals are injured.

One good fortune for Jessie was that she was taken to a clinic where no one wanted to put a healthy dog to sleep. Good common sense! Maybe Jessie's life was taking a complete turn for the better at this point because another good fortune was that she was lying injured and helpless during Mama's shift. Mama actually wasn't even supposed to be there at that time, but she promised two co-workers that she would cover for them that evening and the following day. Fate was again in Jessie's favor! She managed to raise her head, stare into Mama's eyes, and bravely wag her tail. With that motion, Mama made a deal with my doctor, Uncle David. She offered to take Jessie to our home and let her recuperate until another home could be found for her if he would repair her left humerus, which is the bone found in the upper portion of the front legs. A stainless steel pin had to be placed in the bone which, with her activity level, was much more conducive for her healing process than an external splint. The only stipulation Mama expressed about housing her was that I had to like her!

As I am known as "everyone's best friend," you can guess the outcome of our first meeting shortly after her surgery was completed. We immediately started running and playing; at the time, we were operating with only three legs each. So home this 9-month-old youngster came with us.

It didn't take me long to start having some second thoughts about my generosity. Although I liked the company, this was one bold, feisty, on-the-wild-side pup who was sorely lacking in manners. I was starting to look forward to her recovery and placement in a new home. After a month, our mama decided that no home, no matter how apparently nice it was, was going to be good enough for Jessie except ours. I have to admit that, by this time, Jessie and I had worked out our differences, and she had accepted me as a wise, older brother whose lead she should follow.

In case you are wondering, my mama always loved the name "Jessica" and, as she now had a beautiful girl with whom to share it, a new name was entered on the clinic's records. And now for the rest of the story...

Ripple Wilson (RW)

A Prayer for Animals

"Hear our humble prayer, O'God, for our friends, the animals, especially for the animals who are suffering; for any that are hunted or lost or deserted or frightened or hungry; for all that must be put to death.

"We entreat for them all thy mercy and pity, and for those who deal with them we ask a heart of compassion and gentle hands and kindly words. Make us, ourselves, to be true friends to animals and so to share the blessings of the merciful."

Dr. Albert Schweitzer

Caring for Your Puppy Pal

Pamela J. Wilson

The 10 Commandments - From a Pet's Standpoint

"1. My life is likely to last 10 to 15 years. Any separation from you will be painful for me. Remember that before you get me.

2. Give me time to understand what you want from me.

3. Place your trust in me. It is crucial to my well-being.

4. Don't be angry with me for long, and don't lock me up as punishment. You have your work, entertainment, and friends. I have only you.

5. Talk to me sometimes. Even if I don't understand your words, I understand your voice.

6. Be aware that however you treat me, I'll never forget it.

7. Please don't hit me. I can't hit back, but I can bite and scratch, and I really don't want to do that.

8. Before you scold me for being so uncooperative, obstinate or lazy, ask yourself if something might be bothering me. Perhaps I'm not getting the right foods or I've been out in the sun too long or my heart is getting old and weak.

9. Take care of me when I get old. You, too, will grow old.

10. Go with me on difficult journeys. Never say, 'I can't bear to watch,' or 'Let it happen in my absence.' Everything is easier for me if you are there. Remember, I love you."

Fitzsimons Army Medical Center, CO
National Humane Education Society magazine

2

Pesky puppy pal parasites can be found almost everywhere, including the digestive tract. We're barking about nasty creatures such as tapeworms, roundworms, hookworms, and whipworms. All of them can debilitate your puppy pal. You can look for tapeworms in your puppy pal's stool (feces); the segments look like grains of rice. Puppy pals get the most common tapeworms by eating another pesky pest, namely fleas. Roundworms are sometimes passed in the stool and look like strands of spaghetti. Young puppy pals can get these, as well as hookworms, from their mother before they are even born. To detect the eggs of roundworms, hookworms, and whipworms, you need to ask your veterinarian to test your puppy pal's stool for them. Any puppy pal can get them by eating eggs that have been deposited on the ground via the stools of dogs infested with parasites. For instance, after a romp in the park, parasite eggs can get pasted to puppy pals' paws; they then might ingest the eggs while licking their paws. They can also ingest the eggs while chewing on grass that has been contaminated with infested feces. Intestinal parasites can possibly cause puppy pals to be malnourished, do poorly, and have signs of gastrointestinal upset, such as diarrhea. Hookworms are even more sinister in that they suck blood and can cause anemia, especially in young or small animals. Fortunately, they are relatively easy to treat with oral medication.

I have a few myths to dispel at this point in my parasite presentation. Although the nasty worms mentioned above can be shared with people pals, don't fall for the story line that we also give kids pinworms. People share this parasite with members of their own species, so that's one parasite problem you can't pin on us! Another fable is that ringworm is an intestinal parasite when it is actually a zoonotic skin fungus. It causes scaling in patches frequently the shape of a ring. Some folks are relatively resistant to it while others are quite susceptible. Although this fungus among us can be passed from puppy pals (or more commonly kitty cats) to people, it can also be spread to a person by direct contact with an infected person.

Heartworms, which are spread by mosquitoes, are not so simple to treat. As their name indicates, they are found in the heart. They need to be diagnosed via a blood test and, if they are present, treatment is extensive and not without possible complications. However, preventing heartworms is easy by giving your puppy pals medication; consult with a veterinarian so you can pick whichever product and schedule work best for you and your puppy pal.

RW

Puppy Pal Pointers: Attend to puppy pals' health needs; get them checked regularly for pesky parasites.

If puppy pals eat grass, are they sick? Do they have worms? Possibly, but not definitely! This is an issue similar to "Which came first, the chicken or the egg?" Puppy pals sometimes eat grass simply because they enjoy it. Then, because they are not ruminants (like cattle) and cannot digest the cellulose in grass, they vomit what they can't process. Through eons of evolution, puppy pals have learned that, if they eat grass, they probably will vomit. So, if their stomachs are upset (for instance, when they have worms or bacterial or viral gastrointestinal infections), they may possibly eat grass to vomit and relieve the nausea.

If your puppy pal is difficult to medicate, pill time can be turned into treat time. Due to illness, Frisky Wilson had to receive three pills a night. That was a lot by anyone's standards. In those days, dog pills looked like they were meant for a horse, not a 35-pound puppy pal. At the same time every evening, our grandpa used to wrap Frisky's pills in cheese. Then he would hide them in his hands and play the old shell game; Frisky would have to tap Grandpa's hands with his paw to select the one containing the treat-covered pills (of course, he was never wrong). He was a real Quick Draw McPaw when it came to selecting the correct hand! Frisky enjoyed and expected this ritual so much that, when the number of pills he needed decreased, our grandpa still had to provide him with three cheese balls every night, even if some were placebos. Frisky would then wash them down with a cool drink of H_2O fresh from the bathroom faucet. He'd stand on his hind feet, plunk his front paws on the edge of the sink, and lap water that Grandpa would let flow like a fountain over his cupped hands.

Puppy Pal Pointers: Reduce the stress of medicating puppy pals by wrapping pills in treats, such as cheese, to help the medicine go down!

RW

"Just a spoonful of sugar helps the medicine go down in a most delightful way! - *Mary Poppins*, Walt Disney, 1964

"What share we most - we two together? Smells and awareness of the weather. What is it makes us more than dust? My trust in him; in me his trust." - Siegfried Sasson, *Man and Dog*

While we are on the topic of being a responsible pet owner, be sure to establish a preventive health care program for your puppy pal with a veterinarian. Don't neglect to get your puppy pal vaccinated against all the diseases the veterinarian recommends. In most areas, rabies vaccinations are required. Don't put your puppy pals in the position of being on the lam from the law; get their rabies vaccination status updated on a regular basis. Remember, though, that there are many other vaccines available to keep your puppy pal from getting sick, such as distemper, hepatitis, leptospirosis, bordetella, parvovirus, coronavirus... Whiskerchew! Quite a list and quite a mouthful! Makes you *paws* to think about all the diseases we puppy pals can contract.

Believe me, I was never a big advocate for shots. They bothered me as much as the next dog. The good thing was, I never had to spend much time in a clinic waiting room in woeful anticipation of receiving vaccinations because Mama got preferential treatment due to working there. The bad thing was, our mama used to bring the dreaded sharp things home with her and make a sneak attack on what should have been safe, hallowed ground! Nonetheless, when I would hear her tales of puppies, especially youngsters, dying harsh deaths from preventable diseases, I took my medicine with minimal fuss. It was amazing, though, that moments after the torture, I forgot all about it and asked that a second helping be added to my food dish.

It might be advisable to get a puppy pal with an adult size that is manageable for you to lift if necessitated by injury or illness. With Ripple's lanky build and my petite figure (we weighed in the arena of 30 to 40 pounds each), it was easy for Mama to pick us up and carry us to the car or the clinic in an emergency. This was not the case with all the clients of the clinic where Mama worked. In some situations, if nobody was available to assist them with lifting a large dog, they would be stranded at their house with their debilitated pal, unable to transport the impaired critter to the clinic for veterinary aid.

Puppy Pal Pointer: Show your love for your puppy pal. A moment of discomfort can prevent a diminished life of disease and despair. Remember to get your puppy pal vaccinated regularly as recommended by a veterinarian!

JW

"The best doctor is the veterinarian. He can't ask his patients what is the matter - he's got to just know." - Will Rogers

"For disease control efforts in a given population, those who don't vaccinate depend on those who do." – Bill Wilson (teacher extraordinaire)

The Vet

"Viruses and bacteria may infect your pet;
They can cause diseases, that is a sure bet!
FeLeuk, distemper, and parvo, along with rabies,
Are lurking about waiting to infect your animal babies.

It's your responsibility to protect the health of Fido or Fluffy,
By taking them to your veterinarian for checkups annually.
The doctor will look them over, and physical will do;
If they need vaccinations, that's the time to get those, too.

De-worming and flea protection, if needed, are available;
These help your pets feel well and be all that more lovable.
Your pet's doctor can also help if your critters are intact;
Neutering will prevent unwanted kitties and puppies, that's a fact!"

James L. Alexander, DVM, MPVM
(a veterinarian and poet)

"You want your veterinarian to get to know your dogs while they are healthy so he/she can spot changes that can be indicative of health problems later. Your dogs will also be more at ease with your veterinarian if they meet him/her when they are healthy and not in need of so many procedures." - Ann Olsen

Did you know that puppy pals can carry germs that can be dangerous to people and make them sick? It sounds crazy, but it's true, even if we are best friends to people. These germs can be bacteria, viruses, or fungi (hey, I've been known to be a fun guy at parties!). Some are common and some are a rarity. Some can be shed when a puppy pal defecates and the pal may not even appear to be sick.

Diseases passed between animals and people are called zoonoses. Some of these can be a big threat to the health and well-being of both puppy pals and people. You've probably heard war stories about the old days when puppy pals weren't routinely vaccinated against rabies. Rabies is a virus that infects any kind of mammal and is fatal to animals and people without proper and timely treatment. The virus is transmitted in saliva, usually through a bite from a rabid animal. The virus can make you mean and aggressive toward other animals and people, hence the term "mad dog" was given to rabid puppy pals. We're lucky to be living in this day and age when it is easy and affordable for critters to be vaccinated against the rabies virus.

People aren't likely to get sick from touching or owning a sweet puppy pal. To be on the safe side, though, the most important thing people can do to protect themselves from getting sick is to thoroughly wash their hands with running water and soap after contact with puppy pals, their saliva, or their feces.

Puppy Pal Pointer: It's the germs, not the puppy pals, that can be dangerous to people; learn about bacteria, viruses, and fungi and how to protect yourself and your puppy pals against them.

RW

"A person's age and health status may affect his or her immune system, which increases the chances of getting sick. People who are more likely to get diseases from dogs include infants and kids less than 5 years old, people who get new organs, people with HIV/AIDS, and people being treated for cancer." - Rodney Rohde, MS, SV(ASCP)

Mama was always checking Jessie and me for fleas and ticks. She sometimes drove us crazy doing the "flea check" as she and Auntie Carol called it. In Texas, it's almost impossible to have a totally flea-free pet. All you can do is keep the problem to a minimum. Mama had witnessed dogs and cats of all sizes and ages die of flea anemia because their owners did not realize they were covered with the sinister blood-sucking pests. Young critters or very small ones, though, are particularly susceptible to this fate. Fleas also can transmit tapeworms and various diseases such as plague and murine typhus. Even as adults, some animals (and people too) are more attractive to fleas than others. Additionally, animals can be allergic to these nuisances and get itchy, sometimes flaky skin because of them. A veterinarian can help combat this problem, plus perform an evacuation of any hyper-secreting anal glands (which I hesitate mentioning because it is definitely not any puppy pal's favorite medical procedure!).

I was the easy case to treat. My coat was so thin that you could see a flea running amuck. I can verify this because I would stare cross-eyed at any stray flea that wandered up my long legs if Mama happened to miss it on her patrol. Jessie was the one who presented the challenge. Her fox-like coat was so thick that it took forever to wet her thoroughly during a bath, let alone getting the soap through to the skin and then rinsed. The problem with using flea shampoo is that it really doesn't leave a residual protection against fleas. Natural products that were recommended to repel fleas, such as adding brewer's yeast to the diet, didn't seem to make a dent. So when my mama discovered a special flea spray that was safe to use with the flea pills that were being poked down our throats, she thought it was the answer to our problems. (In our younger day, the ingenious flea-control drops that are easy and stress-free to apply on the skin were not yet available. Ask your veterinarian about the newest, most effective products available.) I didn't enjoy it, but Jessie hated the spray so much that she once hid underneath an overturned wheelbarrow in the back yard when she just saw the bottle in Mama's hands. I suspect it wasn't the act of spraying that bothered her as much as the fact that it left you with a sweet aroma while Jessie's idea of perfume was Essence of Dead Toad or Eau de Toilette de Poisson!

In spite of all these efforts, one day Mama noticed Jessie scratching her ears. She decided to use a fine-toothed flea comb around her head for a quick check. Low and behold, Jessie was loaded with the juiciest fleas Mama had seen in a long time! Even in an area where Jessie's coat was at its thinnest, they had managed to hide in mass numbers. They are sneaky bloodsuckers! Boy, did that send waves of guilt throughout Mama's body! War was initiated and won with flea spray, pills, and house and yard treatment. Keep in mind that there are various species of fleas; many live in the surrounding environment and only jump on a passing critter for a meal. That's why it is important to treat where fleas reside throughout the house and yard. To be on the safe side, even the kitties got more anti-flea treatment than their usual flea collar renewal. At least witnessing the cats endure a similar flea-spray torture was a rewarding high point for Jessie! By the way, never use flea products approved only for dogs on your cats. If a product is not approved for cats on the label, it could damage the liver (kitties lack certain liver enzymes that metabolize toxins), potentially leading to the death of your kitty cat.

Ticks are other blood-sucking foes that can transmit diseases such as Lyme disease and ehrlichiosis. One day Auntie Carol noticed Jessie intently following something on the floor. The mighty huntress was tracking an engorged tick trying to make a fast getaway. I guess Jessie knew it was taking a piece of her with it! You can help reduce the number of ticks in your environment by eliminating their habitat. Remove piles of wood around your abode where pests can prosper; this includes not only ticks, but also rats and mice that can harbor fleas.

One other pest that targeted Jessie was biting flies. They are attracted to dogs with prick ears, and as Jessie looked like a small German Shepherd, she had two very appealing pinna. Once they were able to bite and get the pointed ear tips bleeding, more flies would follow in search of a meal. Sometimes poor Jessie would go from lying in a restful slumber in the yard to wildly galloping in an attempt to escape the onslaught of these tenacious buggers. The veterinary clinic, fortunately, had an ointment designed to come to the rescue in just such an occasion!

Puppy Pal Pointer: Watch out for puppy pal pests! Treat your yard, treat your home, and treat your puppy pal against fleas and ticks.

RW

Some types of fleas can deposit up to 25 eggs per day and more than 1,000 eggs in a lifetime. Flea eggs can hatch within 2 to 21 days; a generation, which includes four stages of development, can be completed in 2 to 3 weeks. Fleas can breed from 2 weeks to 2 years (fascinating flea facts provided by Paul Fournier and Glenna Teltow, Texas Department of Health).

Tell*tail* evidence that your pal has fleas includes finding black grains of what appears to be dirt in the coat. Fleas suck blood and then defecate this "flea debris." If your pal gets damp, such as lying on a moist surface, the dry grains will rehydrate into pinpoint-size dots of blood.

Everyone knows that I was always a big believer in good personal hygiene. My mama used to say that I must be part cat, as I would meticulously lick myself if even a drop of mud splattered on me. People have even stopped Mama while we were on a walk and commented on how nice it was to see a dog who kept so clean! I, unfortunately, cannot say the same for my kid sister. Whenever we would go to the lake, she would go out of her way to roll on decaying fish and decomposing algae that were strewn on the shore. Although Mama would try to rinse her off by tossing rocks in the lake for her to retrieve via diving for them, it didn't cut through the foul aroma (being a connoisseur of chicken, I could have at least endured it if it had been a fowl aroma!). When we would load into the car, I would implore Mama with my big brown eyes, which were starting to water from the stench, to make Jessie ride on top of the car instead of in the back seat, but she never heeded my wishes. It was enough to make your tail curl; the things I had to endure!

To be honest, I didn't care for baths and still hesitate to admit that they are a necessity. I would be patient throughout one, though, and just sit with a pitiful look on my face the entire time. However, the scented allergy shampoo Mama used on me did leave me smelling extremely fresh, and my mama snuggled with me all the more after my bath (if that were possible!). If your puppy pal has dry skin like I did due to allergies, you should ask your veterinarian about special shampoos that can help improve this condition and how often to apply these products. After all, you don't want to make the skin even drier by too many baths!

To nobody's surprise, Jessie hated baths. She would display the most doggone woebegone face imaginable. To top it off, with her thick coat thoroughly wetted, she looked like a starving stray. She could barely stand the minutes required to let the flea shampoo do its job, plus her rinse-off time took twice as long as mine (that's one advantage to having a nearly bald belly!). Of course, flea shampoos only killed the fleas that were on her and left little protection against incoming flea attacks. She hated it even more if Mama tried to give her a change of atmosphere by bathing her under the garden hose or in Jessie's Mr. Turtle pool; Mama could really lose control of her outside. Guess Jessie preferred the soothing lukewarm water of the tub, which was better for her than the cold water of the hose. Plus, a wading pool should be associated with fun times, not bath time. The thing I didn't understand was, hours after having a bath, Jessie had no fear of getting her paws wet and would be totally geared to take a swim in dingy, stagnant creek water. Somehow the concept of enjoying water did not overlap to the bathroom, and she did love to have that earthy aroma!

Puppy Pal Pointer: Even though it involves splashing in the water, it's hard to make bath time fun for puppy pals. Try to sing to them, talk to them, or otherwise distract them from the reality of being in a tub instead of a cool pool.

RW

"Anybody who doesn't know what soap tastes like never washed a dog" - Franklin P. Jones

"Bath - a process by which humans drench the floor, walls, and themselves. You can help by shaking vigorously and frequently." - Doggy Dictionary

Take precautions if you bathe your puppy pal outside. Mama knew of several incidents in which pals were lost forever because their collars and tags were removed prior to a bath. The puppy pals, getting excited or upset over the bathing experience, then managed to escape from their yards without any form of identification on them.

Keep water fresh in wading pools; change it at least once or twice a week. Stagnant water is the perfect environment for mosquitoes to breed and their larvae to mature. Mosquitoes can transmit a wide array of diseases to you and your puppy pal.

Sorry, my fellow puppy pals, but good dental hygiene must also be discussed. I know I seem like a traitor to my species with my talk about the importance of taking baths and brushing teeth, but I can't help it. Our mama instilled these concepts in me.

Bad teeth don't just produce bad breath. Plaque can cause receded gums, loss of teeth, and infections. If teeth get severely infected, they can cause systemic health problems, including adversely affecting the kidneys and heart. So when we reached middle age, Mama would schedule us for a yearly teeth cleaning. These went pretty smoothly, but we had to be sedated to enable our doctors to do a thorough job. As we got older, Mama didn't want us to go through the sedation process if it wasn't absolutely necessary. By that time, some great teeth cleaning products had entered the market. There were toothbrushes with long handles for a better reach and toothbrushes that fit on fingertips in order to gently apply toothpaste with the human touch (you could substitute a gauze pad for the fingertip brush). There is toothpaste designed specifically for use in dogs; you don't want to use people toothpaste in puppy pals because it can upset their digestive system if they swallow it. I personally preferred the malt-flavored paste, while Jessie opted for chicken-flavored. I think her preference was simply to please her friends along our walk route. Sometimes after a brushing, we'd stroll down the neighborhood alleys with Mama. When we'd stop for Jessie to flirt with any male dogs on the other side of the alley fences, she would smile and let out a "hhaaa" sound along with a wisp of breath. They would turn their noses upward in sniff mode as if to say, "Hello, Jessie. My, don't you smell delicious? Just like chicken."

Puppy pal pointer: For good health and hygiene, brush your puppy pals' teeth. After all, you want them to be able to enjoy all their favorite meals for years to come!

RW

"Remember, you only have to brush the teeth you want to keep." - Tommy Koenig, RVT, Bert Dodd, DVM (Decker's dentist), and Gary Rassner, DDS

There wasn't one Wilson "sibling" who wasn't homeless prior to adoption. Decker's kittenhood tale is a classic example of indifference and inhumane activity. He was dumped by his owner at a remote lake where he had to take matters into his own paws and fend for any scraps of food he could find. He stayed in the same spot week after week waiting for his owner to return for him. After spying him there a few weeks in a row, Mama used a can of food as bait, picked him up, loaded him into our car, and took him home. Believe it or not, there are imbeciles who believe that, if you place a domesticated animal who has never provided for itself next to a body of water and some woods, it will be able to survive. To these folks I say, "Don't justify your spineless actions with this myth! Your puppy pal, your kitty cat, or even your bunny rabbit will be frightened, starving, and wondering why you so heartlessly abandoned it. Grow up and own up to your responsibility to another living creature." Woof! Don't even get me started on this touchy topic! Have I been dogmatic enough about it?

Not everybody does their pet disposing in the woods. Oftentimes, people who are not such pals to their puppies think they should not be held accountable if they deposit their critters on the steps of an animal clinic. Sure, this is more humane than totally abandoning them. In my opinion, if you do this you need to realize that you are leaving somebody else with your responsibility. Gonzo was a large, wire-haired puppy who was brought to the animal clinic after he was hit by a car. While receiving intense hydrotherapy and treatment to aid him in healing after bone surgery, he continued to develop into a dog of solid girth. His owner never returned for him and left the responsibility of covering treatment costs to the folks at the clinic. Not to worry, as Gonzo had a happy ending and only lost two toes along the way as a result of his accident! First, he went to live with Aunt Anne's mom, Simone. Being a petite older woman, it became slightly dangerous for Simone to try to walk Gonzo, as she could have just as easily ridden him! He then journeyed to friend Lesley's house where he lived a full, happy, and content life. Interestingly, the clinic folks later saw Gonzo's owner's picture in the paper; he was bound for jail. Guess his general lifestyle fit with his irresponsible behavior toward Gonzo.

Uncle David had a good insight on the issue of expecting an animal clinic to provide free care and a home for a puppy pal that is being discarded. When folks would say that they were at least being good Samaritans by depositing the critter at an animal clinic, he would remind them that the good Samaritan of religious fame also left money with the inn keeper when he was helping a poor soul find lodging! The least they could do was provide a little monetary dognation to the rescue cause!

It's no wonder that with histories such as these, Mama insisted that every animal who entered her yard be neutered (castrated for guys and spayed for us girls). It became a joke with Mama's male co-workers that they were afraid to give her a ride to her home for fear they would endure a similar fate! It's estimated that if you start with one male dog and one female dog, they can, over the course of seven generations, initiate the creation of 4,372 puppy pals all in need of homes. That's a lot of puppy tails in the making; I get tired just thinking about it. Mama has been known to state that parents who wanted their children to witness the miracle of birth by letting their dogs and cats have litters should also take their kids to a nearby animal shelter so they could witness the reality of death. Pretty harsh words, I know, but I think we can all understand why she was so emphatic.

There are also health perks associated with neutering puppy pals. Spaying females, a procedure called an ovariohysterectomy, helps to avoid potential uterine infections and, if done early in life [preferably before their first estrus (heat)], reduces the chances of them developing mammary cancer. Additionally, if a female is spayed, she won't go into estrus and attract males from large distances and all walks of life. Castrating males diminishes fighting (including subsequent injuries and infections), roaming, and, in cats, the dreaded art of marking territory through spraying. By the way, neutering male or female puppy pals will not make them fat and lazy, nor will it decrease their guarding instincts. Ripple and I could sound the alarm with the noisiest of pups whenever something was out of sync in our neighborhood. Plus, I kept my foxy figure and Ripple maintained his lean shape for a lifetime even though we were both neutered before we celebrated our first birthday. It helped that we were big believers in good exercise, which tends to keep you physically fit!

There was also an issue raised periodically about men who did not want to have their male dogs neutered. Some type of macho thing, I guess, or they internalized it and put too much of a personal connection with it. (Mind you, I'm not saying all men have such out-of-touch thoughts, especially the kind ones who have touched my life.) Mama sometimes wondered if these same macho men performed gutless-wonder acts such as abandoning dogs in the wild, drowning litters of puppies, or shirking their responsibilities by leaving at the local animal shelter the lives they allowed to be created. Woof to those cowards! Maybe it's appropriate that approximately 70% of the primary caregivers of pet dogs in America are women!

Puppy Pal Pointer: Be responsible; improve and save lives! Get your puppy pals neutered.

JW

"And homeless near a thousand homes I stood, and near a thousand tables pined and wanted food." - William Wordsworth

"The sad fact is that just in the 10 seconds or so that you've been reading this answer, a dog and a cat have been put to death at a shelter because no one wanted them. Irresponsible backyard breeders contribute big time to the pet overpopulation problem. These are people who may mean well but just breed a pet for 'the experience.'" - Steve Dale, *Peoria Journal Star* (when asked by a reader where a male dog could be found for breeding purposes)

In the United States, there's a real pupulation explosion occurring. More than 2,000 dogs and 3,500 cats are born every hour; 47 million dogs and cats are born every year in addition to the 110 million that already exist. The American Humane Society estimates that 15 million dogs and cats will be euthanized per year because they are unwanted (statistics courtesy of Furry Friends - Burt's Bones, Burt's Bees, Inc., Raleigh, NC 27612).

Go to our "Pet Care for Kids" section for a version of Decker's story, *A Cat for Jessie*, to share with young folks. It discusses responsible pet ownership in terms they can understand.

Mander was very faithful to Uncle Randy and Aunt Melissa and would defend them with all the many mighty pounds of his being. Of course, that bonding developed to its fullest using some necessary disciplinary action. Mander was always contending to be the alpha dog even with his own people pals. With a dog of his size, this could become a dangerous situation, so some training was needed. It took some boundary-setting enforcement from Uncle Randy to instill in Mander that he was not the ruler of the roost, was not the alpha of the household, and was expected to play well with others.

He actually was a true gentledog and never picked a fight with a female. He even would come to their rescue in a pinch. There was the time when he took care of his pal, Gracie. A man who was a stranger in their neighborhood was raising a newspaper to strike this small black dog. As the paper was making its way from above the man's head to Gracie's behind, Mander made a powerful jump and, in midair, grabbed the paper in his teeth and confiscated it from the meddlesome man. Little Annie had a very obvious infatuation of him; she idolized and adored him. (Note: I did not fully understand Mander being polite to the ladies, as I never enjoyed the company of Annie or the array of pups of my gender who lived along my favorite walking alleys. I was never two-faced about it, mind you; I always greeted them with a snarl and, if I could get close enough, a nip on the nose! Hey, they asked for it; they were all overflowing with attitude too!)

Unfortunately, not being neutered combined with being a ladies' dog sometimes caused Mander to disappear and hit the streets roaming for female company. Additionally, any males, no matter what the age, did not set well with him. As soon as one even entered a paw into the same park where he was exploring, he felt the need to squash this pup's peaceful outing with a fight. In Mama's more slender days, at one time being close to the proverbial 90-pound weakling, she could be seen flying on the other end of Mander's leash as he rushed to meet any intruders on his turf. Mander definitely believed it was a dog-eat-dog world!

The one male dog Mander liked, to nobody's surprise, was Ripple. Ripple was very pupular and was everyone's best friend, even Mander's. It helped significantly that Ripple was neutered;

this factor avoided any unpleasant confrontations between the two of them right from the first introduction. Ripple admired Mander and followed his lead faithfully. He always enjoyed jumping and nipping at Mander's leash when Uncle Randy, Aunt Melissa, and Mama would take the two of them for a constitutional. One time, Uncle Randy finally caved and playfully gave Ripple (all three legs and 40 pounds of him) the leash in his mouth and let him walk Mander. What a sight their two frames made clipping down the street! Ripple's heart was big enough to conquer the mightiest of souls!

To every rule, there is an exception. When Grandma and Grandpa got Frisky, neutering wasn't the standard procedure that it is today, so they didn't even place it under consideration. Fortunately, Frisky naturally had a gentle personality. He accepted all critters, great and small, with an open mind and heart. Akin to Ferdinand the Bull, he would rather sniff the petunias than participate in a fight!

Puppy Pal Pointer: Avoid conflicts; get puppy pals neutered. Neutering makes them more content to stay home and less likely to roam!

JW

Based on a study in Texas, it appears that neutering males reduces the risk of serious attacks or bites on people by more than two times. Additionally, 78% of female dogs and 90% of male dogs involved in severe bites to people were sexually intact. - Jane Mahlow, DVM, MS, Texas Department of Health

Generally, neutering will take the edge out of your male puppy pal's fight. It always amazed me, though, how kitty cats (even neutered ones) could still get purulent abscesses from sharp, nasty nails that pierced their bodies during a fight. Granted, they wouldn't fight to a deadly level or develop fight pads in their cheeks like old warrior tom cats, but they would still get the pus forming and flowing. Even sweet, mellow Tater would, from time to time, return home with a funky wound. One time, Mama had him on the exam table at the animal clinic while she flushed a facial abscess. Tater was so gentle that he let Mama do this all by herself, which is almost unheard of in the kitty cat world. Usually, it takes a minimum of two people and the occasional shot of anesthetic to do this procedure. As Tater was lying on the table taking his medicine, Sam, a skinny, black and white clinic cat, put his paws on the table and, with one of them, patted Tater ever so gently on his face. It was as if he were saying, "It will be OK, Tater." I guess even cats have their moments. By the way, people pals should care for their pets by trimming their nails and getting their cats scratching posts. Sometimes those nails can get so long that they curl around and grow into the pads. Ouch! (Hey, what am I complaining about? At least they can't scratch me if their claws are otherwise indisposed.) As for puppy pals when their nails get too long, it's hard for them to get adequate traction when walking on smooth surfaces. They then can be injured when they slip and slide.

On another occasion, Mattie developed an abscess; it was on the top of her head. Our usually demure, sweet-natured Mattie would turn into a banshee as soon as she was carried into the clinic, and she definitely needed a few sets of hands on her tiny body for the treatment ritual! As the wound was being flushed with Betadine and hydrogen peroxide, Mama noticed that the frothing fluid was flowing straight through and exiting near Mattie's chin. We were all wondering if Mattie was lacking matter in her head to prevent this free flow of fluid through it. Poor Mattie, the if-I-only-had-a-brain joke was started that day for her and stuck.

Speaking of Mattie, she lived up to her name. Her long hair was always getting humongous mats in it; she was very vocal about not wanting Mama to comb her. Keep this in mind whenever you get long-haired puppy pals too. They need constant assistance with their grooming, including being brushed or combed on a regular basis to keep mats from forming. Ripple and I couldn't really relate to this dilemma because we preferred low-maintenance hairdos; we kept our coats short, soft, and clean.

There were several incidents in which a dog or cat was brought to the clinic where Mama worked to get mats shaved. Remember, you can't trim these hair clumps with scissors because they are too close to the skin; you're almost sure to snip the skin by accident, and the critter will need stitches. Periodically, the deciding factor for a person to finally bring the pet in was not so much the animal's appearance as it was the poor being's odor. This odor was occasionally accompanied by a swarm of maggots that had taken up residence beneath the mats. Flies don't just deposit eggs on decaying matter. They'll lay them on live tissue if it's in an area where the animal can't reach or keep clean. This also sometimes happens to critters who are "down in the hind" (not ambulatory) and have gathered urine and feces on their coats, which serve as magnets for maggots.

Puppy Pal Pointer: Commit time on a regular basis to groom puppy pals. Develop a routine for trimming their nails and brushing their coats.

JW

Flies can start laying eggs in batches of 75 to 150 within 4 to 20 days of becoming an adult. Within her lifetime, a female fly can deposit approximately 500 eggs; these eggs then hatch within 12 to 24 hours (fascinating fly facts provided by Paul Fournier and Glenna Teltow, Texas Department of Health).

When Mama first got Ripple, she fell into the young-and-dumb category on certain aspects of puppy care. With his faithful help, she learned a lot about owning a puppy pal. For instance, although she knew to keep the family dogs, Frisky and Annie, on a leash at all times, being in a free-spirit, college atmosphere tempted her to have a more carefree attitude about Ripple's restrictions. It didn't seem right to her that he shouldn't be able to walk with her unconfined and with the ability to roam. Mind you, Ripple always stuck near her and even patiently waited outside stores while she went shopping. At least Mama didn't buy the mythical malarkey that, once a dog has been hit by a car, he'll never let it happen again because he now has a fear of cars. I used to lunge at motorcycles with a vengeance years after my automobile accident! Still, Mama fought the idea of always having him on a leash.

One day they were walking along an extremely busy street when Ripple spotted a squirrel across the road. Squirrels were his nemeses (mine too!), so he didn't even look one way, let alone both ways, before crossing the street. By the time he decided the squirrel was beyond his reach and was doubling back to Mama, he suddenly realized that a blue blazer was on a collision course with him. The driver must have seen Mama's frantic hand waves, because he slowed just enough to allow Ripple to drop and roll to the side of the left front wheel; he amazingly emerged unscathed. Ripple saw his life flash before him at that moment and seconds later when Mama was hugging him to death. Whenever she thought about the years she would have been without him due to that one instant, the leash never seemed too restrictive again. She also learned the safety value of setting boundaries for those growing under your guidance, be they kids or puppy pals.

Puppy Pal Pointer: Plan on spending a lifetime with your puppy pals; keep them on a leash along those city streets.

JW

"To man the greatest blessing is individual freedom; to a dog it is the last word in despair." - Author Unknown

"It is tough grounding your puppy pal, but that is what ruff love is all about." - Pamela Baty (protector and caregiver to all critters)

In her fledgling years, Mama was too little to walk Frisky by herself. Even so, she knew that he needed to be on his leash at all times while outside so he could not run away and get lost. One day, her sage older sister, Auntie Carol, walked Frisky with the intent to tire him and then handed Mama his leash so she could just stand in the yard with him. All was going smoothly until Auntie Carol took the notion to run down the sidewalk like a crazy kid calling to Frisky to chase her. Being a pup who minded well, he did as he was instructed. In a flash, Mama was flying behind him holding tight to the reins. However, because she was a young tyke, she tripped and was soon body sledding on the cement sidewalk, still refusing to let go of the leash with Frisky's safety in mind. When the bumps and thumps of the wild ride came to a close, the skin had been stripped from her knees and tops of her feet. Grandma was so pleased with Auntie Carol's antics. Oh, the joys of learning lessons in childhood!

Years later after a few learning experiences in which Mama almost lost me to a set of car tires, she once again became very diligent about keeping her dogs within her reach, be it via a leash or a fence. For the home situation, Jessie and I had the best of both worlds, including a fence for when we wanted to play in the back yard and a lead attached to a stake in the ground for when we wanted to survey activities from the front yard.

On one memorable morning shortly after we had moved into a new home, Mama was on the phone chatting with Auntie Carol. She was looking out our window sharing the neighborhood excitement with her, as a woman walking down the street was being harassed by a little reddish-brown dog. It suddenly dawned on Mama that the pesky little dog was, in reality, our own rowdy Jessie who supposedly was safe and secure in the back yard! Mama dropped the phone and ran to the aid of the woman. Before the woman had a chance to give Mama what appeared to be a well-deserved lecture on allowing out-of-control dogs to roam, Mama apologized profusely to her and explained that she was new to the house and there must be an unbeknownst hole in the fence. That was how we met our neighbor, Barb, who grasped the situation and gave us all a fresh start (after all, first appearances can be deceiving). We all soon became very close friends, and I always barked my loudest and happiest when she stopped to visit during one of her neighborhood walks.

Here's another doggone story. During one of our daily constitutionals combing the alleys of the neighborhood, Mama spotted the skinny rear ends of two dogs, one tall and one small. Although they were a block away, she recognized those rumps immediately. They belonged to Aunt Joyce's Greyhound, Jade, and her Whippet, Elsie. Mama cut our walk short and took us home (don't worry, we made sure she made up for it later) so she could capture these escaped scamps. It seems that they had also found a magic window of opportunity to depart from their fenced yard.

On yet another walk from the park one day, Mama suddenly realized that an animal control truck was following us. We were on leashes, so no problem there. However, when curious dogs left their front porches to investigate us, they were apprehended. Mama felt like we were being used as bait in some dragnet. She tried to warn intrepid dogs to return to their yards, but it was to no avail. Finally, we jetted down an alley, and the truck lost our trail. Mama has a lot of respect for animal control personnel and the stressful, thankless jobs they face; she even helped with designing and implementing a statewide training program for them. True, also, that for their own safety, these pups shouldn't have been left loose to approach the road. She still didn't want to be part of this sting operation, and neither did we!

Mama felt lucky in that Jessie and I were content and did not try to find escape routes from our enclosed yard. We know when and where we have it good! Some pups spend all of their free time with this mission in mind. Take, for example, Frannie; I guess her Heeler instincts gave her the drive to want to comb the streets searching for lost sheep. This escape artist could find a pathway out of any fence. She must have had a Guardian Angel with her during her escapes because she always managed to find her way back to her abode or someone was kind enough to assist her in finding her way home.

Of course, the key was always having tags on a collar that would not readily slip from her neck. Not only did Frannie have a rabies tag with her veterinarian's contact information (name, address, and phone number) on it, she also had a city tag in case she was placed in the animal control facility during one of her adventures. That way, even if the clinic was closed at the time of her capture, the diligent folks at animal control had a mechanism for locating her family. In addition to a collar and all these tags, even a harness was soon necessary for this pup who worked doggedly while on a regular leash to back out of her collar and continue to earn the nickname "Francini Houdini." One thing you can try if you have an escape artist like Frannie is to extend chicken wire from the bottom of your fence and bury it beneath the ground; it should help prevent your puppy pal from digging out of the safety of the yard.

Speaking of tags and collars, if you put a collar on a small pup, be sure to check how snug it feels as the youngster grows and buy replacements as needed. Collars have actually been found embedded in a growing dog's neck, which causes discomfort and possibly severe damage to the skin and muscle.

By the way, we have a word of warning if your puppy pals behave like Frannie. Take care if you put them on a rope or chain in a fenced yard. Make sure the rope or chain is short enough so they can't reach or climb the fence. Uncle Bob once shared a tragic, but true, story about his dear dog, Sheba, who loved to climb the fence. Most unfortunately, Uncle Bob returned home one day to find that Sheba had climbed the fence, but because the chain fastened to her collar was too short to reach the ground on the other side, she had hung herself. Our hearts cringed for him when we heard this sorrowful tale.

Puppy Pal Pointer: Ensure that your pals can find their way back home. Tag, tattoo, or microchip them so your eyes can behold their beauty once again.

RW

According to the National Humane Education Society, five million pets are reported missing each year; it's a sorrowful feeling to have them disappear and never know their fate. You might want to contact a humane society, an animal control agency, or a veterinarian for information on how to tattoo (usually in the inner rear leg) or microchip your puppy pals. It could help prevent them from being added to this sad statistic. If you have a microchip implanted in your puppy pal, make sure the chip is compatible with scanners at local animal control agencies and veterinary clinics. Even with a tattoo or microchip, it would be wise to use collars with tags on your pets as sources of quick, easy identification for anybody who happens to find them.

Like most of us, Abbie Ladd liked to explore the neighborhood. When her family first brought her home from the animal shelter, she was naturally anxious to check out the local action. That proved to be a big mistake on her part. Will these pups ever learn how good they have it and just stay put?

Although her back yard was completely surrounded by a fence, it didn't take her long to discover a small opening between the garage and the fence on the property line. Even though she was a medium-sized girl (not petite like me!), she managed to squeeze through the opening and find her way to Freedomsville.

John, who now shared his heart, home, and family with Abbie, spied her trotting through the neighborhood having a grand time. He tried to catch her, but he wasn't nearly fast enough; so the dance of Abbie's dogtrot continued to a busy intersection. That's when the accident happened; tires squealed as Abbie collided with a car and skidded down the pavement.

You can open your eyes now because this story has a happy ending. After a trip to an animal hospital, plus X-rays and shots of all kinds given in every imaginable part of her body, she was able to return home. The fence, in the meantime, had been sealed. After all, a secure fence and a gate probably won't cost as much in the long run as a two-night stay in the animal hospital. Plus, it will certainly save you worry and grief over your puppy pals and prevent pain and suffering on their part.

Puppy Pal Pointer: Keep fences in good repair; don't allow your puppy pal the opportunity to hit the road.

JW

"All I could think about while skidding along Magnolia Boulevard was, 'Maybe I should have stayed at home.'" - Abbie Ladd

You never know when your puppy pal might be injured in an accident or unintentionally ingest something toxic. If you live in a town that has an emergency animal clinic, add the number and address to your emergency contact list along with a poison hotline number. You might also drive to the clinic prior to any real emergency to make sure you know where it is; then you can get to it quickly and with less stress during an actual crisis. If there is not such a clinic nearby, discuss with your veterinarian what his or her policy is for receiving after-hours calls and handling emergencies. Additionally, buy or prepare a first aid kit and purchase a book about first aid for pets; place both items in a location that will be readily accessible to you in a crisis.

It was a warm, fine day for January. Mama was working the afternoon/evening shift at the animal clinic, so we spent the morning running errands with her. First, we took a walk around the neighborhood; then we enjoyed a trip in the car to the grocery store with a subsequent pit stop at Auntie Carol's house. Finally, home again to play while Mama unpacked the groceries. What happened next went so fast that I'm still not sure of the details. Ripple collapsed on the living room floor right in front of me and started to seizure. I really wasn't sure what to do, so I started barking in a high-pitched frenzy and biting at his head in an attempt to get him up. Let it never be said that I don't remain calm and collected during an emergency! Fortunately, Mama rounded the corner from the kitchen to see what was causing the commotion and came to my aid. Next thing I knew she was loading Ripple in the back seat of the car. I didn't see them again until the next day. In the meantime, I joined a slumber party with my cat cousins, Ketra and Cato, at Auntie Carol's house that night.

The following day I learned that I had almost lost my big brother and best friend. Ripple had spent 18 hours on an IV at the clinic. Mama and Uncle David had held a vigil over him all through the night. It was soon discovered that some truly evil coward in our neighborhood had laid bacon grease laced with strychnine all over the ground, and Ripple unwittingly had grabbed a bite of this deadly recipe on our early morning walk. As an eerie realization after this event, Mama remembered that when Ripple snatched a scrap of food from the ground before she could pull him away, she had thought, "My luck, it's probably poisoned." This was a strange coincidence, or maybe instincts kicking into gear, because Mama usually was not one for processing such negative thoughts. If Mama had left for work before he had started to seizure, she would have come home to a tragedy. The one good thing pertaining to a strychnine incident is that, if an animal's body doesn't collapse from the seizures and survives the poisoning, there are no detrimental, long-term side effects.

Unfortunately, as we later attempted to alert the neighborhood to this atrocious, inhumane act, we discovered that other dogs had not been so fortunate. We were told by folks that they had arrived home to find dead dogs in their yards. We also concluded that it was somebody's attempt to teach a lesson to a few dogs who were getting in trash cans. Instead of discussing the problem with the poor dogs' owners who were responsible for their actions, this pathetic coward dispersed a toxic substance where any animal or child could contact it or ingest it. Illegal - yes. Immoral - yes. All we could hope was that the long arm of the paw would eventually catch up with this spineless person and that karma would be returned in kind someday.

Puppy Pal Pointer: Be aware that not everyone is a pal to your puppies. Keep a watchful eye on your puppy pals, and try to prevent them from encountering a hazard or eating one!

JW

"Until he extends his compassion to all living things, man will not himself find peace." - Dr. Albert Schweitzer

"It's just a little old-fashioned karma comin' down; just a little old-fashioned justice goin' round. It really ain't hard to understand; if you're goin' to dance, you gotta pay the band." - Willie Nelson,

Little Old-Fashioned Karma, Tougher Than Leather, Sony Music Entertainment, Inc., Columbia, 2003

"If a dog will not come to you after having looked you in the face, you should go home and examine your conscience." - Woodrow Wilson

One Christmas a group of us went on a long journey to transport Auntie Carol from Illinois to her new home in Texas. The cab of Uncle Jeff's old blue and white pickup truck was filled with passengers, so special arrangements had to be made for me and Uncle Jeff's dog, Briar Jack (aka B.J.). Uncle Jeff built us a wood dog house and placed it in the bed of the truck. He lined it with down sleeping bags because the December air promised to be quite chilly, especially when adding the wind-chill factor that came with moving on the highway. B.J., being a real outdoorsy kind of dog (aka "a nut"), rode the distance with his head peering over the side of the truck; his whiskers were quickly covered with frost. As for me, I didn't budge from my warm, cozy house until we arrived at a rest stop. I only stuck my long, slender nose out the cloth door flap in order to bark at gas station attendants; nothing could motivate me to join the winter air. In retrospect, we were very lucky that B.J., not being as careful or as wise as me, did not take a tumble and suffer an injury, especially on the interstate.

Not all travels have such worry-free results. In Scappy's early months of life he didn't have quite the sturdy build that he later developed. Story has it that one day his dad (we'll call him "Straw") was trying to be a good pal to his puppy. He loaded little Scappy in his pickup truck and took him to the animal clinic to get his first round of vaccinations. After this was accomplished, Straw and Scappy began their short, but memorable, journey home. As Straw looked in his rearview mirror to check on Scappy, the little black body disappeared. You guessed it, the tyke had fallen out of the bed of the truck. To Straw's dismay, he was immediately returning to the animal clinic, but this time it was not for a routine visit. Scappy had a broken leg. A splint and six weeks later, Scappy fortunately was ready to once again run with the big dogs.

Mama has seen much worse than that. One puppy pal was brought to the clinic with all the pads torn off his feet, plus multiple scrapes and bruises over his body. His owner thought that, by tying him to a chain, his puppy pal would not be able to abandon the truck. Sadly, the chain was just long enough to allow the poor pup to jump, and then he was dragged by the very person who cared for him. As tragic as this sounds, it could have been worse; at least he was still alive. Some puppy pals suffered a similar fate but did not survive to tell the tale. In some of these instances, unchained puppy pals would, when the truck hit a bump, fall out of the bed and be hit by their owners' truck or the car on the road behind it. In yet another sad tale, some old family friends were once passed by a truck with a dog hanging from the back; the poor soul was dead, of course. It made for quite a horrific vision.

Puppy Pal Pointer: A lot can happen even in a short journey; do not let your puppy pal ride in the bed of your truck!

RW

"Seen a man standin' over a dead dog lyin' by the highway in the ditch. He's lookin' down kinda puzzled pokin' that dog with a stick. Got his car door flung open he's standin' out on highway 31. Like if he stood there long enough that dog'd get up and run. Struck me kinda funny seem kinda funny sir to me. Still at the end of every hard day people find some reason to believe." - Bruce Springsteen, *Reason to Believe, Nebraska*, Columbia Records, 1982

Accidents can happen in the flick of a tail. Picture another scene featuring that cute little red-haired girl, Frannie. As the story goes, her "Francini Houdini" personality once again overrode her common sense. On what should have been a relaxing trip to Webberville Park, she and her canine siblings, Choco and Scappy, were safely stowed in the back of Straw's Subaru wagon. He had learned his lesson about not letting dogs ride in the back of a pickup truck after the incident in which Scappy broke his leg after hitting the pavement. Now you may think to yourself, "How could anything possibly go wrong? She's safe and secure in an enclosed car, and the windows are cracked open just enough to allow the pups to catch some scents on the breeze." Well, you obviously don't know Ms. Houdini!

An ice cooler in the back of the station wagon had overturned, and Straw was afraid Frannie would start chewing the gel pack that was now available to her. As he didn't want her to tear open the pack, he pulled off the four-lane highway which, of course, was enduring the height of five o'clock traffic. With his whole body blocking the side door while he leaned in the car to collect the spilled cooler contents, Francini Houdini still managed to squeeze over his shoulder and run right for the road. In her mind, they were stopped at the park and she was ready to romp. She was on a definite collision course with a car pulling a trailer. If it didn't hit her, it seemed inevitable that the car running parallel with it would. Somehow, she slid past the first car and stopped just shy of the second car. Whew! Then she continued across two more lanes of traffic to a grassy field. For a moment, a look on her face indicated that she recognized she had made a big error, especially when she realized that the other Straw dogs were not by her side. What happened next would make you freeze in your pawsteps. She made the hasty decision to clear the four lanes of traffic one more time and return to her pup-pack pals. By this time, Straw was running through the middle of traffic frantically waving his arms. A Guardian Angel was following this pup once again because all the leading cars in each lane simultaneously stopped to allow her to cross! I guess the lesson here is that, even when you are doing everything right, an outing can go terribly wrong.

Mama remembered a sorrowful incident in which a girl, scheduled to have her cat spayed, entered the animal clinic in tears. As she was traveling along the interstate on the way to her appointment, her cat had squeezed through the slightly cracked car window and disappeared. I'm sure this kitty had a Guardian Angel, too, but the outcome was just destined to be different. Mama had also heard stories from clients of this same occurrence happening as they were moving across country or taking a trip. Their stressed-out kitties had managed to slip through the smallest window opening imaginable and were never seen by their owners again. Kitty cats really tend to travel better, and with fewer disappearing acts, if they are confined in a carrier where they feel secure and more in control of their surroundings. I guess these poor little critters don't enjoy an outing in the car like Jessie and I do. Come to think of it, I don't recall our kitties ever begging Mama for a ride, which was a tactic we maneuvered with perfection!

Puppy Pal Pointer: Be wary of potential disasters when traveling with your puppy pals. Be cautious when opening car doors and windows.

RW

"It's a long dark highway and a thin white line, connecting baby, your heart to mine. We're runnin' now but darlin' we will stand in time, to face the ties that bind, the ties that bind. Now you can't break the ties that bind. You can't forsake the ties that bind." - Bruce Springsteen, *Ties That Bind*, *The River*, Columbia Records, 1980

Our times with Uncle Jeff were always great fun; we shared pawsitively the best of times with him! He knew how to get on the floor and really play like a puppy. He even played tug-of-war with an old, holey T-shirt using his teeth, just like us! We also enjoyed ruffing it when we went camping, rock climbing, swimming, and canoeing with him. Even Ripple, who was clippy-clopping on only three paws, relished these excursions.

When Uncle Jeff moved to the northlands, he started to raise sled dogs. This husky team of thick-coated dogs became known as our Canadian canine cousins. We thought they must be such lucky dogs to spend their days playing with Uncle Jeff.

Now don't get us wrong; we had no desire to trade places. It's true that, when I had a chance to romp in the snow, I loved to leap through snow drifts, grab snowballs in flight with my mouth, and burrow my nose under the snow in order to get all the delicious scents. I, though, had a lustrous, thick coat. Ripple's almost hairless belly would not have faired well in that wintry climate just as the sled dogs' dense coats would not have been comfortable to them during Texas summers. Although a trim could provide relief, completely shaving these thick-coated dogs because they have been placed in a warm climate for which they are not naturally suited is not particularly a service to them because their coats also provide an insulated cooling system for them. Plus, shaved dogs left outside with no shade can get a sunburn just like people can. (We don't recommend this practice for any puppy pal, shaved or not, as all of us can suffer or die from heatstroke if not provided with adequate shelter.) Last but not least, the shaved style of coat is not a good look for most puppy pals, and it's sure to bring a few snickers their way! This is why you need to choose your puppy pals based to a certain extent on your living environment, including your yard and house size, to meet their physical and behavioral needs.

The first member of Uncle Jeff's team was Tanner. As a side tale, one of our favorite stories to bark about was from Tanner's puppyhood. Uncle Jeff had entered the two of them in a local sled-pulling contest in Minnesota, where Uncle Jeff worked at an Outward Bound. Even though they were supposed to be a team, we puppies had an inkling as to which one of them would be doing the majority of the work. Anyway, the streets were lined with spectators as Uncle Jeff and Tanner approached the center stage. As Uncle Jeff started to check the equipment, he heard laughter starting to flow through the crowds. When he looked toward his sled, Tanner was sitting in it eagerly awaiting a ride with Uncle Jeff serving as the lead dog! Now that's our kind of dog! It was reminiscent of the classic scene in Dr. Suess' animated *How the Grinch Stole Christmas*, in which the Grinch's dog, Max, jumped in the sled seat with the anticipation of a fun-filled ride, not realizing that a work-laden trek was before him. Woe be it to anyone who tries to force hard labor on us. After all, with working our tails off tending to duties such as guarding the house, supervising kitchen activities, and barking at the mailperson and garbage/recycling collectors, who has time for additional toils?

Puppy Pal Pointers: Puppy pals are designed for different tasks and environments. Make sure you keep your puppy pals' comfort zones in mind when choosing their living arrangements.

JW

"Cats are smarter than dogs. You can't get eight cats to pull a sled through snow." - Jeff Valdez

"Never work during rest times and take plenty of rest times." - *For Women Who Do Too Much*, Workman Publishing, 2000

"My sled dogs are half pet and full work dogs; they have been trained with love and never asked to do anything I would not do in equal effort. Tanner once pulled a 200-pound load (I had a 70-pound pack) for a 3-week trip in minus 30-degree weather conditions. For both of us it was our vacation and an easy trip; he zigzagged all over the lakes and the only scare was when he chased an otter toward an open water hole! Such is the strength of these dogs." - Uncle Jeff

You, too, could have astonishing adventures with Uncle Jeff filled with dog sledding or canoeing. He and his pup pack run Voyageur and Klondike Ventures in Alberta, Canada. We highly recommend them and give them two paws up!

According to the US Department of Agriculture's Animal Welfare Act, you need to provide adequate shelter to protect animals from any cold or inclement weather and direct effects of wind, rain, or snow.

"Keep indoor pets in a dry, warm area free of drafts. If possible, elevate your pet's bed off the floor. Provide outdoor dogs or cats with a dry, insulated pet house or shelter out of the wind. Bring your pets inside if the wind-chill factor or other weather conditions become severe. Staying warm requires extra calories, so feed your pet accordingly when the temperature drops. Talk to your veterinarian for advice on feeding your pet." - Ralston Purina Company

When Ripple was a youngster, he used to keep pace with the fastest of the big dogs. He'd run circles in games of high-speed chases and used his stump as a pivot; sometimes he almost caught me! He even tried his paw at rock climbing with Uncle Jeff, Mama, and their good friends, Steve, Dave, Mike, and Jeri. "Fat Man's Squeeze," a hill crevice in Shawnee National Forest, was a favorite during Ripple's college days at Southern Illinois University. On one such adventure, Steve's foot became wedged in the passage because there was no bend to his steel-toed boots. As everyone was teasing him for getting stuck and he was complaining about how nobody could make it through such a narrow space, Ripple, who had rollicked his way around the hill, doubled back through the Squeeze and passed right over Steve on his way out! Is that the recipe for how you rub salt in a wound? It wasn't intentional on Ripple's part; with his kind heart, he didn't know how to purposely hurt a guy!

When Ripple indulged in a swim, people used to do a double take when he would come running out of the lake and they suddenly realized his limp was actually the sign of a missing limb. Ripple's spirit certainly was unstoppable.

When he got a little older and arthritic (a condition even more difficult with which to cope if you only have three legs), Ripple needed a lift getting into the front seat of the car, but Mama was always glad to oblige. Additionally, the long walks we both loved to take could sometimes take their toll on him by the following day. Mama got to the point where she would pay money to drive into our favorite place at Decker Lake so Ripple didn't have to walk the extra trek from the parking area outside the gate. When the kind folks who worked there realized she was just taking us for an outing and not going boating or fishing, they decided to let her enter for free. How's that for some good hearts? Of course, our irresistible personas probably aided them in making this generous gesture! We so enjoyed trotting through the yellow, red, blue, and pink wildflowers in the field next to the lake. One thing Ripple found that really soothed his aching arthritic bones after these romps was a calm swim in the lake. It was so relieving for him to dog paddle quietly in the water, turning in slow circles where the water was not too deep. He'd be so content that he would slip into a dog daze of summer. Ah, it didn't take much to please that dog!

Puppy Pal Pointer: Provide your older puppy pals with physical therapy to relax them, comfort them, and meet their needs. Exercise is good for puppy pals just like it is for people.

JW

"Allow the experience of fresh air and the wind in your face to be pure ecstasy." - Author Unknown

"Nobody can be in good health if he does not have fresh air, sunshine, and good water." - Flying Hawk, Ogala Sioux Chief

"He was a joy to me when I met him as a young dog. He only had three legs, but he could wag his tail with the best of them." - Great-Aunt Nan Wilson (commenting on her first encounter with Ripple)

Whenever Mama left on a trip, she made sure Aunt Diana, Uncle Vern, or some other favorite family friend was responsible for taking care of us. We always encouraged her to leave detailed instructions and treats with them by either refusing to eat or demonstrating some sign of illness as soon as we saw the suitcases appear. These actions also served to intensify her feelings of guilt about leaving us.

On one particular trip Mama made to New Orleans, she placed Uncle David on duty. She had left a gift box of pastries for him (as if just having the honor of taking care of us wasn't reward enough!) on the kitchen butcher block. Now we happened to note the exact location of this box because, when Uncle David stopped by to check on us over the noon hour, he shared a chocolate éclair with us. He left to return to work, and we had no idea if he was going to come back to take care of us! It was only natural that our survival instincts and teamwork capabilities kicked into high mode. Ripple's aching sweet tooth reminded him where the box of delicacies was stashed, but his three-legged status prevented him from reaching them. I, on the other paw, was quite agile. Enough said, as no one except us has ever known exactly how the great pastry spill* occurred, and we aren't spilling any more details. When Uncle David finally appeared, milk carton in hand for a session of pastries and *The Andy Griffith Show*, he was stunned to find that the pastry box was lying empty on the kitchen floor. There wasn't a crumb to be found (at least we were extremely neat about the whole thing). The only evidence that remained of the existence of those pastries was a thin coating of powdered sugar remaining on the floor from a plump cream puff. Poor Uncle David, if he had only reassured us that he was going to return, we wouldn't have been forced to unite forces and pursue such desperate measures. Fortunately for everyone involved, we didn't suffer any gastrointestinal upset after enacting this survival scenario.

It has been reported that dogs sometimes hide their food because of instinct. They are merely following traits of their wolf forefathers, who hid leftovers during a feast phase so sustenance awaited them during a famine phase. Ripple once had to resort to this primitive mannerism while on vacation at the beach with Mama and Auntie Carol. Those two had the audacity to leave Ripple alone in a hotel room while they went to feed their faces at a seafood restaurant (you guessed it: they saw food, and they ate it!). Not knowing what food the future would bring him, Ripple sprung into action. By the time Mama and Auntie Carol, stuffed to the gills with fish, finally returned to the room, Ripple had doggedly "buried" Milk-Bones** by shoving them into every corner of the room. Once again, an example of a puppy pal relying on his instincts and acting in quiet desperation in the light of desertion!

Puppy Pal Pointer: Puppy pals have strong survival instincts and know how to apply them well; it's your duty to ensure that they don't have to resort to such desperate measures.

JW

"Dogs love company. They place it first on their short list of needs." - J.R. Ackerley, *My Dog Tulip*.

The Animal Hospital Association has found that 76% of owners feel guilty about leaving their pets at home, plus 50% leave out toys and 32% turn the TV or radio on for their pets when they leave (courtesy of the 1999 *365 Dogs Calendar* by Workman Publishing).

* The great pastry spill became a legend in our family. When Mama wrote her children's book, *Tales From Tubblewood: A Duck For All Seasons*, she even named a store in downtown Tubblewood "David's Doughnuts" after dear Uncle David.

** Milk-Bone - a product of Nabisco, East Hanover, NJ 07936

Even though this is a book about puppy pal pointers, there are times when a cat's tale is so exceptional that we need to give it credit. Mona, who shared his abode with our friends, Renee and Dave, set one such example. (Don't let the name confuse you. Mona is a male kitty cat. As is often the case, it is hard to tell the sex of these confusing critters, especially when they are young. It is not uncommon to meet a female cat named Carl or a male cat named Mona!) In this story, curiosity really did almost kill a cat. Mona gambled with exploring an open door and almost didn't live to tell about it. Below is his tale, which we'll let Aunt Renee tell in her own words.

"In 1987 Mona and I moved to an apartment complex away from the downtown area. He took the move well, although there weren't any open apartments in this complex for him to visit. He made regular trips to the pool and stayed close to our apartment. He did develop a new jumping routine. Again, I was on the second floor; this time with a balcony. I'm not quite sure how he ever got off the balcony, but you can imagine my surprise one afternoon when I looked out the window and came face to face with a cat in a tree! I watched as he leapt from the tree branch onto the balcony.

"In 1989 I thought my heart was going to break. Mona didn't come home. I couldn't believe it at first and would glance anxiously up at the balcony every time I drove into the parking lot. There continued to be no Mona waiting at the door. Soon I was putting those pitiful missing cat signs around the neighborhood. I waited for an entire week. No Mona. On the eighth day I took the day off of work thinking I had the flu. By midmorning I felt pretty good and decided to go down to the laundry room and run a few loads of wash. When I reached the bottom of the stairs, I heard a faint meowing sound. I stood frozen with my basket of towels. I pinpointed the direction of the sound; it was coming from the apartment that was below the one I lived in. I couldn't understand this because I knew the people that lived there. They did not have a cat, and they had left for vacation in Florida a week ago. It all sunk in quickly; I ran to get the manager to look inside the apartment. Within ten minutes she went into the apartment and came out carrying a fluffy, slightly skinny Mona. I could not believe it. He had reverted back to his old habits of going in open doors, and this time no one noticed him. He had been left behind when the residents happily rode off to Florida unaware they had an unwanted guest. I carried the poor cat up to the apartment where he drank a very large amount of water. His veterinarian was shocked that he had made it out alive; I was glad to finally know what had happened to him."

Puppy Pal Pointer: If your puppy pal is missing, check with neighbors and call your local shelter; also post signs and place announcements in local newspapers and websites that advertise lost pets. When looking for a lost kitty, remember that they could have been accidentally shut in a nearby garage or storage building.

JW

"For push of nose, for perseverance, there is nothing to beat a cat." - Emily Carr

"Because of our willingness to accept cats as superhuman creatures, they are the ideal animals with which to work creatively." - Roni Schotter

"If man could be crossed with the cat it would improve man, but it would deteriorate the cat." - Mark Twain

A clinic client told our mama that he had thoroughly searched his neighborhood for his lost cat. He finally thought to enter a neighbor's garage and take a look. There, sticking out of the lid of a washing machine, was his cat's tale. The critter had jumped into the machine and the lid had accidentally closed. Fortunately, both the cat and the tail were still in good repair.

We don't know Annie's exact history, but when Grandma and Grandpa adopted her, she was leery of men. Uncle Jeff used to lie face down in the grass with one arm extended so she could cautiously approach and investigate him. Before long, she, like the rest of us, adored Uncle Jeff. Her puppyhood was so traumatic that she was afraid of jack-o'-lanterns and birthday cakes with the candles lit. After seeing a photo with Frisky happily behind his birthday cake right in the middle of the family festivities, her fear made a sad statement about her roots and the abuse she endured during her formative months. Annie did get revenge of sorts. Her former owners used to live across the street from Grandpa and Grandma.

Every time they were out and about, you could hear Annie growling at them from her perch on a bed by a window upstairs.

Although I was abandoned by my owners after my car accident, Mama still thought they must have had some merit. After all, they had several kids who seemingly encouraged me to love everyone. Sure, Snoopy wasn't a creative name for a white dog with black patches, but at least they tried. Jessie's owners had at least one child. Whatever happened to her in her puppyhood caused her to be aggressive toward children the rest of her life. Dubbing her with the name Dumbsh-- on her medical record did not speak well of her owners and did not give her much of a self-image. It's hard to live up to your potential with so much negativity bestowed upon you from the start. Additionally, at 6 to 10 weeks of age puppy pals undergo a socialization period. It is critical to handle these youngsters properly, instill trust in them, and teach them to interact with family and friends during this time. After 14 to 16 weeks of age, they may never have the social skills to intermingle with other beings.

Abuse, be it physical, verbal, or emotional, affects puppy pals for the rest of their lives just as it does people. Although we dogs may not understand every human word that is said to us, we are sensitive to tone of voice. We can tell if you are angry, stressed, excited, or happy. Remember this when you're forming a relationship with a new puppy pal or when you go home at the end of a hard day. We give our love unconditionally; shouldn't we expect the same from you?

Puppy Pal Pointer: Teach kids the importance of respecting and caring for all living beings. Never abuse your puppy pals physically, verbally, or emotionally. Instead, learn lessons from them on how to practice unconditional love.

RW

"If you do not step on the dog's tail, he will not bite you." - African Proverb

"If you pick up a starving dog and make him prosperous, he will not bite you. This is the principal difference between a dog and a man." - Mark Twain

"The question is not 'Can they reason?' nor 'Can they talk?' but 'Can they suffer?'" - Jeremy Bentham

It has been found that violent acts toward animals are often precursors to other forms of violence toward people. If you witness someone mistreating an animal, do not take it lightly. React and, if necessary, report them for the welfare of that animal and for the future safety of the next potential two- or four-legged victim.

For parents who laugh at their tot who is abusing an animal and condone it because he is just "being a kid," remember that the child who abuses an animal today becomes the Jeffrey Dahmer, David Berkowitz (Son of Sam), or Albert DeSalvo (Boston Strangler) of tomorrow. When, as children, they abused animals, they were not reprimanded because it was thought that they would simply outgrow this supposed phase of childhood (excerpt courtesy of Anna C. Briggs and Constance Clark, *Because We Love Them...A Handbook for Animal Lovers*, National Humane Education Society, 1994).

There are Federal laws that address animal cruelty, plus many states have laws that pertain to this issue. In Texas, depending on the offense, the penalty for various forms of animal cruelty can range from a Class A misdemeanor to a felony of the 3rd degree. Texas law also requires counseling for children who practice acts of cruelty toward animals.

Teach kids how to care for their puppy pals. Do not indulge the philosophy that, because they asked for a puppy pal of their own, they are to be solely responsible for caring for the critter. Kids need assistance and guidance from adults on how to properly care for puppy pals, including providing them with fresh water and balanced meals on a daily basis, grooming, exercise, a warm, dry, comfortable place to live and sleep, and regular visits to the veterinarian.

Mama used to rehabilitate orphaned or injured wild animals. It seemed like we always had guests, be they squirrels, pigeons, grackles, or blue jays. We even had Walter Pigeon and Atticus Finch among our famous group of wounded boarders. We were frequented most often by baby squirrels. When Ripple encountered squirrels in his back yard or at the park, he viewed them as antagonists. As he would charge at them, they would calmly finish eating the pecan in their paws before ascending the tree. They weren't worried in the least about being caught during one of Ripple's ferocious three-legged advances! However, when he heard orphans squeaking for their supper or saw Mama feeding them, it was like he had a maternal instinct for them. His brow even developed a worried look as he supervised Mama while she tended to them. Even I, who was dubbed "the most horrible" because of my interactions with other critters and children, would show concern for these babies when they cried. If Mama was sleeping and I could hear their distress, I would pace and whine until I woke Mama so she could meet their needs.

Mama made sure that Ripple and I didn't have too much contact with these tiny creatures. Although she knew we were interested in them, she didn't want them to get used to any puppies. She explained that, once they were released in the wild, she didn't want them to trust people or puppies. After all, not everyone was as kindhearted as we were! She made sure that they could eat food from the wild before she let them go solo. She took time to locate good places for them to call home; available food and water were musts, and, to be on the safe side, a low cat and dog count was desirable for their new habitats.

One special squirrel trio, Winkin', Blinkin', and Nod, came to us with their eyes still shut. Although Mama regretted it when they went from depending on her for their bottle feeding to stamping their feet as an alarm on top of their cardboard box home as if she were the enemy when she entered the room, she knew that it was the way it should be. I think that she secretly wished they would still trust her but know enough to be wary of the rest of her kind! Other sweet squirrels who graced our lives until they were released were Fergie, named for her radiant red hair, Crazy Squirrel, who came to us in a wobbly state following a head trauma, Dean-O, who was originally rescued by our good friend, Dean, and Cass and Michelle, who were California dreamers!

Of course we will never forget Peapod, a flying squirrel who was dropped off as a baby by clinic clients from the piney woods of East Texas. This little guy was a hoot to watch, and he provided us with endless hours of entertainment. He even arranged his cage to suit his discriminating tastes. For instance, he used an empty half of a pecan shell as a bowl. One day he set a peanut in his pecan bowl. Another day he removed the peanut and replaced it with a piece of watermelon Mama had brought him from her brunch outing, so it was now a lovely fruit bowl. Mama really wanted to keep him, but after having a dream in which our mellowest kitty, Tater, captured him, she remembered that wild animals belong in the wild. Peapod was transported back East to live with a protected colony of his peers so he could have his own friends and family, plus learn the laws of the jungle.

Puppy Pal Pointer: When caring for any living creatures, make sure you do what is best for their health, survival, and quality of life.

JW

"All things bright and beautiful, all creatures great and small, all things wise and wonderful, the Lord God made them all." - Cecil Frances Alexander [We highly recommend the inspirational books having these same names written by a true pal to puppies everywhere, Dr. James Herriot (Bantam Books, NY). He's a veterinarian from Yorkshire and one of the people (along with Jacques Cousteau and Jimmy Stewart) that Mama admires most.]

"With all beings and all things we shall be as relatives." - Sioux Indian

Don't try this at home! Mama saw a cat attack a juvenile squirrel. She was able to scare the cat away, which allowed the young squirrel time to scurry to safety and collapse in a tree hollow. Mama got on a ladder, held a big towel outside the hollow, and gently coaxed the dazed squirrel into climbing onto her covered hands. She was, indeed, a squirrel whisperer. By the time she got him into a carrier and transported him to the clinic for treatment, he was beginning to surface from his stupor and was none too happy. After treatment and recuperation time, he was returned to his home in the trees for another happy ending. In retrospect, Mama was lucky that this little guy didn't jump across the small space between their faces and attach his teeth to her nose instead of submissively crawling onto the towel!

OK, so enough about what you can do for your puppy pal. Sure we depend on people to care for us and help keep us in good health, but we also do the same for people. Therapy dogs provide a pawsitive presence in nursing homes, centers for the mentally ill, and hospitals. Patient health benefits created by these pals include promoting activity; improving mobility skills, communication, and memory skills; helping patients forget about their pain, loneliness, or boredom; providing a warm body to touch, stroke, hug, and offer treats; filling the void felt by patients missing their animals at home; giving a sense of being needed; putting long-lost smiles on faces; and restoring spirit to the lonely. Just 30 minutes a week with one of us cute puppy pals can reduce loneliness for these patients. We're so good at it that it's been given the fancy name of animal-assisted therapy, which is free to boot!

Many animals also have a sixth sense about a person's mental or physical condition, and they can alert staff members to these problems. Having a pet has demonstrated significant benefits for sufferers of Alzheimer's disease by lowering anxiety in these patients. Some dogs have even been known to detect melanomas, a type of skin cancer, that may have otherwise gone unnoticed. There are also wide arrays of assistance dogs who commit their lives to helping people with physical disabilities. How's that for being service-oriented?

And what about us non-service dogs on the home front? We help the elderly too. In our own back yard, Jessie brought a smile to the face of our neighbor, old Mr. Cone, and raised his spirits. As he was trying to place an aluminum pie pan filled with table scraps over our fence for both of us to enjoy, Jessie grabbed the rim of the plate with her razor-sharp teeth and sped off like a flash with it. Now I don't want to put my paw in my mouth and call anybody "selfish" (did I mention that the treats were for both of us, doggone it?!), so I'll just let you think it. Anyway, the point of my story is that, every time Mr. Cone would tell Mama the tale of Jessie and the pie pan, he would start laughing (the best key to staying young that there is) and thoroughly enjoy the memory of it all, even if I didn't see the humor in it!

Critters in general can stimulate you to react to stressful people and situations in a more constructive manner. They can also help you achieve your endeavors. Take a horse named Pal. He was a wonderful companion and true friend to Beverlee. In her words, "Pal helped focus my academic studies and my career in veterinary medicine. More importantly, Pal was always there for me. He carried me when I could not walk, he consoled me when no humans could, and he taught me through his spirit and wisdom."

Pets are known to be wonderful healers (and we aren't just referring to that cute little red Heeler named Frannie!) of the psyche. Puppy pals have been known to lower blood pressure in people merely by their physical presence. By petting a pup for 10 minutes, you can reduce your blood pressure and increase your mood-elevating chemicals. We just might lower your cholesterol too. We make excellent napping partners and encourage you to relax and get adequate rest, which is good for your overall health. We puppies also will get you off the couch and out walking to inhale the fresh air and enjoy the changing seasons, plus burn calories and lose weight. Now that's classic exercise at its best!

Puppy Pal Pointer: To quote one of Mama's favorite song lines, "Old dogs care about you even when you make mistakes." - Tom T. Hall

RW

"If your dog is fat, you aren't getting enough exercise." - Author Unknown

"There is no psychiatrist in the world like a puppy licking your face." - Ben Williams

Some researchers at Brooklyn College indicate that coronary patients who owned dogs were eight times more likely to survive at least one year after their heart attacks. - Amy I. Attas, VMD, *Good Housekeeping*, March 2002

Spike Olsen is one of the hardest working dogs in the feel-good business. He's been a volunteer with Therapy Pet Pals for five years. Once a week he's on a mission to lend a helping paw by visiting residents and staff of a nursing home.

He is recognized by one and all when he enters the building. The staff enjoy his visit because he provides a refreshing, fun-filled break in their routine. They are kind enough to always have a few treats awaiting him, even though he doesn't expect any pay for the job that he does!

He has a wonderful bedside manner, literally, as he frequently visits patients by sitting on their bed. The comfort they find in stroking this gray ball of fur is the best natural medicine possible for stress relief. He encourages folks who haven't spoken a word to anybody else to chat with him. Some of these folks have no family to visit them, but they can relax and revel in telling Spike stories of their past pets and life experiences. He brings a little bit of home to them. Who could ask for anything more from a puppy pal or any other being for that matter?

Puppy Pal Pointer: If you are looking for an activity to do with your dog, consider an organization like Therapy Pet Pals. You and your puppy pal can reinforce the bond you share while offering friendship and compassion to those in need.

RW

"Dogs are magic. If you don't think so, spend some time with mine once a week." - Ann Olsen (Spike's mom)

Frisky counts his cheese-covered pills from Grandpa; tasty coverings can make it easier to take pills

Many insects like to pester puppy pals; prick ears like Jessie's are targets for biting flies

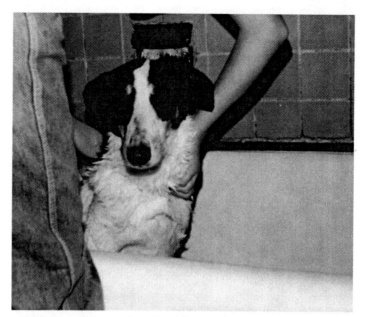

"If I shut my eyes, will this all go away?" Although he doesn't care for baths, Ripple knows they are important to keep his coat shiny and skin healthy

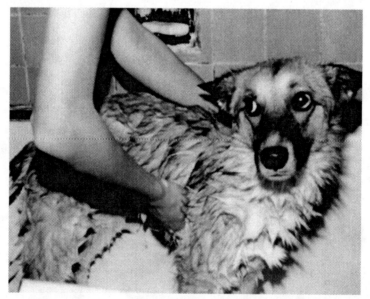

Even though she feels perky after a bath, Jessie displays a woebegone face during the process

Jessie's dislike of bath water did not carry over to her enjoyment of her swimming pool water; always keep water fresh in pools and bowls

Even Jessie's cat, Decker, does not seem to mind spending time in the pool; all critters need access to clean water

Brushing her teeth keeps Jessie's smile bright and breath fresh; clean teeth go paw in paw with good health

Since all of us were adopted as adults, we only have youngster pictures of Tater (provided by his former owner); consider adopting older animals who are in need of a home

Although Tater joined our family as an adult, we discovered through old photos that he had a look of surprise on his face even as a youth

Gonzo had a tough beginning and lost a few toes along the way before he found his happy ending with Lesley; don't abandon your pals when they are injured or ill

Mander is always polite to females like Annie; because he wasn't neutered, he tended to be aggressive toward males

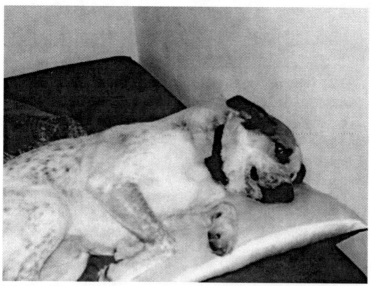

Mighty Mander shows his gentle side to his people pals; discipline and setting boundaries help form solid working relationships and bonding

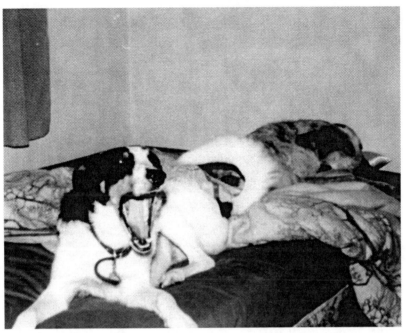

Sleepy Jeepy and Mander are ready for a nap; being neutered helps Ripple mingle with dogs of his own gender and prevents him from adding to the pupulation explosion

Long hair can develop mats; critters like Mattie (seen here rolling on a bed of catnip) need frequent grooming

Jessie demonstrates wearing a collar and identification tags, which are essential accessories for all puppy pals

Ripple is wearing a collar with identification tags to ensure somebody could help him find his way home if he got lost

After Abbie Ladd's car accident, she decided staying home by the fire was the life to lead; mending fences helps to ensure that your puppy pal is adequately contained

After a close call with a car, Frannie learned that it was better to stay with her pup pack than to roam on her own (from left to right: Choco, Frannie, Scappy, and Straw)

Francini Houdini wears a collar and harness to make sure she doesn't stray (from left to right: Choco, Scappy, Mama, and Frannie)

Ripple's eternal young-at-heart energy permitted him to skyrocket through the air and land on Uncle Jeff's lap

Jessie and Ripple like romping in the Illinois snow, but they also enjoy winters in warmer climates such as Texas

Jessie feels frisky around snow, even if it is contained in a glass globe (this activity is supervised to avoid accidents)

Tanner takes the lead of Uncle Jeff's sled and heart (from left to right: Tanner, Rasti, Emily, and Uncle Jeff)

Uncle Jeff set an example and gave his kids guidance on how to tenderly care for their pack of pups (from left to right: Spirit, Phantom, Juli, Tsunami, and Jeremy)

Northern neighbors, our Canadian canine cousins, need heavy coats in their cold climate (Mukluk and Skye with Juli, Aunt Jill, Uncle Jeff, and Jeremy)

Even though Ripple only had three legs, he could rock climb with the best of them; Ripple has much to teach us about courage and spirit

A relaxing swim in the lake helps to sooth Ripple's arthritis and cool the dog days of summer

After leaving an abusive household, a loving environment helped Annie overcome her fears (seen here gingerly investigating Grandpa and Mama carving a jack-o'-lantern)

 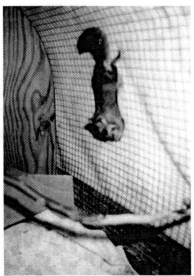

Jessie likes chasing squirrels, but her mothering instinct kicks into gear when she is around their orphaned babies

Peapod, the flying squirrel, was a fascinating addition to our family until he joined his natural peers

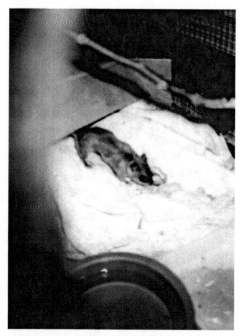

Adorable Peapod liked to arrange his food and habitat; we made sure he kept his wild instincts

Jessie's many duties include keeping Mama company and helping her study; puppy pals enhance mental, physical, and emotional health

Decker is also known to have hit the books with Mama

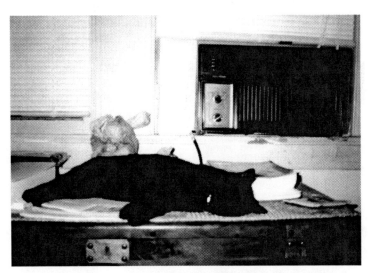

Leave it to a cat to fall asleep on the job

Pamela J. Wilson

Treating Your Puppy Pal

Eighteen Things to Learn From a Dog!!!

1. Never pass up the opportunity to go for a joy ride.
2. Allow the experience of fresh air and the wind in your face to be pure ecstasy.
3. When loved ones come home, always run to greet them.
4. When it's in your best interest, practice obedience.
5. Let others know when they've invaded your territory.
6. Take naps, and stretch before rising.
7. Run, romp, and play daily.
8. Eat with gusto and enthusiasm.
9. Be loyal.
10. Never pretend to be something you're not.
11. If what you want is buried, dig until you find it.
12. When someone is having a bad day, be silent, sit close by, and nuzzle him or her gently.
13. Thrive on attention, and let people touch you.
14. Avoid biting when a simple growl will do.
15. On hot days, drink lots of water and lie under a shady tree.
16. When you're happy, dance around and wag your entire body.
17. Delight in the simple joy of a long walk.
18. No matter how often you're scolded, don't buy into the guilt thing and pout...run right back and make friends.

Author Unknown

The student housing duplex where Ripple and Mama lived was really in abhorrent condition. It had green carpet, orange walls, and burgundy furniture. Good thing dogs are relatively colorblind. Ripple could have gone crazy looking at that mess all day!

Dogs have much better taste than most folks realize. We were continually encouraging our Mama to add padding around the house. As soon as she would set a new rug in a strategic position on the hardwood floor, Ripple would plop right on it. He would demonstrate how much he enjoyed his new look-out post by happily surveying household activities from it. He had learned from a pro named Annie, the old carpet crawler herself. When Grandpa and Grandma got new carpeting for the living room, she kicked her hind legs straight out behind her and started the "alligator crawl" by pulling herself forward with her front legs. There's just nothing like a good belly rub on a fresh, clean, soft surface!

One of our greatest accomplishments was in sending telepathic waves to Auntie Carol and Mama when they went shopping on what they coined a "$100 day." Now they really didn't spend $100, but they treated themselves to buying some items for the house. I think that made them feel like $100! One day they came home with synthetic sheepskin rugs in which even our finicky cat cousins, Ketra and Cato, reveled. (By the way, I never have understood why cats enjoy lying on plain old paper so much; give me a comfy bed or soft rug anytime!) Another time, Auntie Carol draped Mama's bed, one of our main hangouts, with a fresh, plump, dusty rose and white comforter. As soon as it hit the bed, we two puppies were trying it out for size. Ah, the simple pleasures! After noting the look of contentment on our faces, Auntie Carol wondered why they hadn't thought to get us a comforter a long time ago. We, too, were wondering why they didn't have more snap! Auntie Carol then determined that all shopping should be done with us in mind because we appreciated each new addition to the house so much, be it bedding supplies or a cozy rug. Fortunately for all of us, they had wisely learned an important lesson that day!

Mama kept her box spring and mattress on the floor so Ripple did not have to jump too far. This was an especially important feature when he got older and developed a touch of arthritis. Our friend,

Francine, had a different type of solution for her aging chocolate Labrador, Shadow, who suffered from back problems. She had some custom-made steps placed next to her bed so Shadow could easily walk onto the bed instead of having to jump. (When Mama mentioned Shadow's stairs to us, Ripple went into a drooling daze dreaming of an entirely chocolate dog!)

As Ripple got older, Mama bought him "the royal pad," a geriatric friendly pet bed. It had a soft fleece cover that encased a piece of textured foam designed to aid with arthritis. Woof, did he love it. So much so that he would puff his cheeks in discontent and stare holes in me if I ever tried to spend time on it. Not to worry, as there was Auntie Carol to the rescue. She knew how I loved to open packages. Whenever she or Grandma sent Mama care packages, they always included treats in it as a reward for me because they knew I would be the one actually doing the work and opening the box! Therefore, she sent an enormous one just for me one Christmas. My heart skipped with anticipation as I ripped through the heavy cardboard box. Next, I tore and shredded the festive green Christmas paper that enwrapped the large, soft package. Inside was pawsitively the finest blanket I've ever encountered in my whole life! One side had a green southwest motif, but the side I preferred was made of fleece. Mama immediately placed it on the couch, which became my favorite spot in the whole house. I think it was paws down one of the best gifts I have ever received. Come to think of it, I've often heard Mama say it was one of the best gifts that she ever received too. The beauty of the blanket was compounded by the joy Mama got just from watching me open my package with such vigor and delight and from watching my countless hours of napping on my special blanket!

Puppy Pal Pointer: All creatures enjoy creature comforts.

JW

"...not Carnegie, Vanderbuilt and Astor together could have raised money enough to buy a quarter share in my little dog..." - Ernest Thompson Seton

"Every dog should have a man of his own. There is nothing like a well-behaved person around the house to spread the dog's blanket for him or bring him his supper when he comes home man-tired at night." - Cory Ford

When I first joined the Wilson household, I immediately tried to take over. Heck, Ripple was so relaxed that I seized every moment to let him know who was "Top Dog." All was going according to my plan until Mama gave us the chocolate cake pan to clean. That's when it happened. Ripple took matters into his own paws and showed his dominance with one sneer of his lip. After that, my inspiration for share-and-share-alike was heightened.

Mama and I soon discovered that you just didn't come between Ripple and his chocolate. His eyes would glaze over just being in its presence! He became a fiend at Halloween and could smell wrapped Easter candy that was hidden on an upper closet shelf behind closed doors. Uncle David, who lived in a garage apartment a block from us, confessed that he would unwrap the foil from Hershey's Kisses* ever so gingerly because he sensed that Ripple would be able to hear a chocolate wrapper opening at least a mile away!

After Ripple had passionately professed his love for chocolate, Mama read reports that it was toxic to dogs. If I remember correctly, it was something to do with the theobromine in it causing complications. Before she informed Ripple of the travesty, more research was warranted. It turns out the reports were true, so we wouldn't condone or recommend giving puppy pals chocolate. It's a reality, though, that dogs have a propensity for this delicacy, and Ripple's tolerance to small amounts of the tasty substance had been established before the toxicity issues were revealed. Mama always monitored Ripple's intake of sweets because, if left to his own means, he would have eaten pawfuls of cocoa-based goodies. Moderation, as so often is the case, was the key. The less sweet the chocolate, the more toxic it is (can't that be said of us all?!). Unsweetened baking chocolate contains about 8 times more theobromine than milk chocolate.

Mama couldn't stand to think of Ripple spending the rest of his life without something he enjoyed so much, so she found a way to indulge him with this delicacy. She switched to a healthy route with chocolate-flavored vitamins and homemade chocolate dog biscuits she created using a recipe for dogs and a dog-bone shaped cookie cutter. I never did develop an attraction for chocolate, so my favorite homemade dog biscuits were cheese/garlic flavored.

Ripple would wait patiently by the oven while the biscuits were baking so he could be there when they emerged from their toasty chamber. At least he didn't drool on them like Uncle Jeff once did on his birthday cake when, as a kid, he was watching Grandma ice it! Ripple and I had to admit that we admired Uncle Jeff's strategy. After that display of excessive salivation, nobody in the family felt the overwhelming desire to partake in a piece of cake, so there was all the more for him.

Puppy Pal Pointer: To quote one of Mama's old microbiology professors, "A little poison is good for you." (In that particular lecture, the professor was referring to the fact that a low level of exposure to certain viruses and bacteria can help you build a resistance to them. Here we are segueing the concept to refer to moderation while enjoying treats!)

JW

"A little of what you fancy does you good." - Marie Lloyd

"Part of the secret of success in life is to eat what you like and let the food fight it out inside." - Mark Twain

"Drool - what you do when your persons have food and you don't. To do this properly, you must sit as close as you can, look

sad, and let the drool fall to the floor or, better yet, on their laps."
- Doggy Dictionary

The American Society for the Prevention of Cruelty to Animals'
Poison Control Center reported mild signs of chocolate toxicity in
animals eating 20 mg/kg of chocolate and severe signs in animals
eating 40 mg/kg.

* Hershey's Kisses - a product of Hershey Foods Corporation,
Hershey Chocolate U.S.A., Hershey, Pennsylvania   17033-0815

Ever since I started living with Mama, she was a real stickler
for proper diet to an extent! When we were young, she made sure
we had a nutritious, balanced commercial dog food. Milk Bones*
were also pupular with both Mama and us. We liked the flavor, and
Mama liked the fact that they helped to keep our teeth clean and our
breath fresh. She was always excited to try any new dog treats that
hit the market, but she also made sure we got to enjoy some people
food. Whenever she ate under our watchful eyes, she always saved
at least two bites, one for each of us, at the end of the meal. Doggy
bags were remembered, especially from the County Line, a true
Texas-style barbeque restaurant where she would make a request for
all the beef ribs they could spare (pun intended!). Those barbeque
bones were whisker-lickin' good! Although we only received one
bone on a given night, we knew the rest were being frozen for our
future dining pleasure. We didn't get bones of this type very often
because they can splinter and be dangerous for a voracious pup, plus
they might damage teeth. Usually it's best to stick with a chew toy
or a thick, rounded soup bone and stay away from chicken bones.
As the French Poodles would say, "Bone appetit!"
   When people would inform her that she shouldn't be giving
us treats and people food, the example set by our long, healthy
lives proved them wrong. You just need to avoid excess and apply
moderation. Now we aren't barking about folks who pile their

puppy pals' platters high with nothing but rich food, although we
have dreamed of such a life. It's also best to avoid any sudden
changes in the diet (for example, spices, too much fat, or too much
milk) because this might create an intestinal upset accompanied
by diarrhea and vomiting, which none of us enjoy experiencing.
Additionally, there have been the occasional anecdotal reports of
dogs having detrimental reactions to certain people food, so you
can't always assume that just because you can safely eat it, your
puppy pal can as well.

Ripple and I always marveled at the genius of modern
technology. Oftentimes, Auntie Carol and Mama would take us on
a ride to a mystical "food place." There, while just nonchalantly
sitting in our own car, a magical window would open and some
foreign hands would pass food to us, be it hamburgers, chicken, ice
cream, or any assortment of yummy sandwiches. What will they
think of next?

When Ripple was in his mid-teens and had a bleeding gastric
ulcer due to arthritis medication, Mama prepared the recommended
bland diet for him, which consisted mostly of Cream of Wheat**
and cottage cheese. It held no attraction for me, but Ripple seemed
to enjoy it. Vanilla yogurt also fared well with him and his tender
tummy. In the mornings during the stint when his ulcer was
misbehaving, Mama would serve him Gerber's*** strained baby
food, including a bottle of ham and a bottle of egg, for a yummy
breakfast. Here's a hot tip discovered at the clinic: strained meat
baby food is attractive to puppy pals and even finicky kitty cats who
are off their feed, and it is easy to digest for those with gastrointestinal
woes. The chicken and turkey flavors always seemed particularly
tempting.

As we aged, Mama provided us with prescription diets for our
various ailments, such as sodium-restricted foods for Ripple's heart
murmur and protein-restricted foods for my sensitive kidneys. Diet
modifications in response to medical conditions are important to
consider; a veterinarian can guide you on appropriate food fare. You
don't want to make food so bland that your puppy pal quits eating.
Mama really delighted in preparing the home-cooked prescription
diets for us; our doctors provided the recipes. After all, we never

complained about the cuisine! Both our routine geriatric diets consisted of different balanced meals of rice and hamburger (or substitute chicken or turkey for a tasteful change). She also roamed the isles of the grocery store looking for tasty, prepared substitutions in order to give us a variety at mealtime. Mama felt that it was the very least service she could provide for us after all the wonderful things we had done for her!

Puppy Pal Pointer: Provide your puppy pals with a menu that is compatible with their age and health conditions. Remember, no matter who you are, a little dessert can make life sweeter.

JW

"Food is an important part of a balanced diet." - Fran Lebowitz

"Ever consider what our dogs must think of us? I mean, here we come back from a grocery store with the most amazing haul - chicken, pork, half a cow. They must think we're the greatest hunters on earth." - Anne Tyler

"She was willing to eat what I made for her - the third day I'd ever baked in my life. And unless she just liked to suffer, she really liked my cooking!" - Dan Dye and Mark Beckloff (co-founders of Three Dog Bakery), *Amazing Gracie*, Workman Publishing, NY, 2000 (totally enjoyable book given as a gift to Mama from Annie Bright)

"If your dog thinks you're the greatest chef, don't seek a second opinion." - on a magnet given to us from Aunt Shannon

"Frannie is on a special weight diet. She sits by her bowl and waits for it to be filled with food." - Straw

Our theory is that Mama believed in moderation of special diets because of Great-Grandma Andersen. She had a gentle heart, but it was not a healthy one. In the last several months of her life, her doctors decreed that she could not have any salt in her diet. Mama remembers her begging for just a shake of salt on her food to give it taste. Great-Grandma Andersen soon no longer enjoyed going out for dinner with her friends because ordering became so difficult and food no longer gave her pleasure. She lost interest in eating in general and passed away. This, to Mama, defeated the whole reason behind modifying Great-Grandma Andersen's diet, which was to enhance and extend her life instead of diminish and shorten it. Although absolutely no salt in her food might had prolonged her life, moderation with a splash of salt might have added flavor to those last few months. Even though Mama wanted to lengthen the amount of time she had with us as much as possible, she took to heart this lesson of balancing quantity of life with quality of life.

* Milk-Bone - a product of Nabisco, East Hanover, NJ 07936
** Cream of Wheat - a product of Nabisco, East Hanover, NJ 07936
*** Gerber's 2nd Foods - a product of Gerber Products Company, Freemont, MI 49413

Ripple was more eccentric with his tastes in food than I was. For a dog, he was a novelty (or a nut, whichever term you prefer) in that he loved vegetables. I'm not kidding; he thought that green beans, corn, and potatoes were just swell. As for me, I had more of "steakholder" interest in meal matters. On holidays when a big feast was served, Mama would serve us our own plates with a bite or two of everything. I counted on Ripple to clean the rest of my plate after I had inhaled, I mean ingested, the meat and gravy portions. Frisky Wilson was even pickier than me. Legend has it that he once cleaned a plate to a gleaming polish except for one pea that had strayed onto his plate, and he even licked the gravy off of it!

Let me warn you that some of our canine colleagues can overplay their paw and get too finicky in their food preferences and demands. Then when those puppy pals are really sick and not eating, it might be assumed they are just being stubborn. This may cause a delay in them being taken to a veterinarian for a true medical problem.

Try to ensure this doesn't happen by keeping your puppy pals on a schedule with a balanced dog food. Dry, crunchy food can also help somewhat with tartar control.

Frisky was very similar to Ripple on one taste issue, which was that they both had an intense sweet tooth. I'd venture to say they had a total of 84 sweet teeth between them. On one hysteric, I mean historic, occasion when Mama was a youngster, the Easter Bunny had just paid the household a visit. When Mama and her siblings were getting ready to leave for church that morning, Uncle Jeff decided to be clever and hide his Easter basket under his bed. After all, if Mama, Uncle Randy, or Auntie Carol made it upstairs before he did, he didn't want them tapping his candy cache. Believe me, this kid had taken inventory down to the last jelly bean! Well, a scene that brought tears to Uncle Jeff's eyes awaited him when he got home from church. Decorating the long flight of stairs leading to the bedrooms was a stream of pastel-colored candy wrappers sans the heavenly treats that they were designed to protect. It seems that Frisky had done some scouting while the rest of the family was in church and discovered the ill-fated Easter basket under the bed. Poor Uncle Jeff! It was a good thing that Grandma had a stash of candy hidden away to assist the Easter Bunny in case such a crisis materialized! Maybe Uncle Jeff's prayers had been answered after all! Another prayer was answered when Frisky didn't suffer toxic side effects from the chocolate.

Frisky made the most of every holiday. Our grandpa loved to decorate the Christmas tree. He had made tinsel distribution into a fine art. He once even followed through on the idea that the candy canes would look better if they were hung on the tree with their plastic covering removed. Frisky sure agreed with him. Without the wrapper, they were much easier to devour after removing them from the tree. That was when Grandpa learned the valuable lesson of not placing anything edible or potentially harmful near the bottom of the Christmas tree. He also discovered that only nonbreakable ornaments belonged in this location, particularly if you have a perky puppy pal who likes to wag his tail.

Frisky, in general, was very resourceful when it came to obtaining treats. One night, he woke Grandma by placing his paws on the side of her bed and clicking a penny between his teeth. Grandma was so worried that he would swallow it and possibly hurt himself that she rushed downstairs to get a cookie to trade for it. Sure, he had to cause a little commotion and stir Grandma from her slumber in order to get a midnight snack, but at least he was willing to pay cold hard cash for it!

Puppy Pal Pointer: Your puppy pals have discriminating tastes; take the time to learn their likes and dislikes so they don't have to take matters into their own paws. Do so with a certain amount of moderation and balance so your puppy pals don't get too finicky.

JW

"My Sampson is more faithful than most Hollywood men I know, and he doesn't care how much I weigh." - Alicia Silverstone

Chocolate is a potential holiday health hazard because it can be toxic to puppy pals; don't leave it where your pal can discover it and be tempted to eat it. Liquid in some snowglobes may contain antifreeze, which can be toxic if ingested. Holiday plants can also pose hazards. Mistletoe, particularly the berries, can cause gastrointestinal and neurological clinical signs, including convulsions. Ivy, Christmas cacti, and poinsettia plants can all cause diarrhea and vomiting if ingested. Whether or not poinsettia plants are toxic has been debated for years. One way or the other, animals tend to be attracted to them, so it's a good practice to keep them out of the reach of curious critters. Additionally, don't leave firecrackers where your pet can access them and be tempted to chew on them with a possibly explosive outcome. (Plant information provided by John C. Haliburton, Texas A&M University, College Station, Texas)

Just for the record, I may have had eccentric tastes in that I loved vegetables (and crisp, fresh June bugs right off the screen door that could only have been more delicious if they had been dipped in

chocolate, but that's another story), but at least I had discerning tastes. Jessie found some of the most disgusting items suited her not-so-sensitive palate; it's amazing that, given her propensity for trash and other such nasty hors d'oeuvres, she didn't suffer from frequent bouts of vomiting and diarrhea. She unfortunately had the illusion that the crunchies she discovered in the kitty cats' litter box were actually candy delicacies. She even raided the diaper pail during a stay at Uncle Randy and Aunt Melissa's place and shredded the contents that lurked within to make sure she got the most pleasure possible from them. Yep, give me a clean plate of vegetables any day!

Having a propensity similar to Jessie's for getting into things she shouldn't almost brought about Frannie Lu's demise. She discovered some rodent poison that was meant for another critter and nibbled on the package. The poison didn't care if a puppy pal or a rodent ingested it; it made Frannie start bleeding to death internally just as it would a rat. If Frannie hadn't been taken to the animal emergency clinic for a late night shot of Vitamin K to stop the hemorrhage and a blood transfusion, her tale would have ended in tragedy.

I did have a few food follies, but none that compared to the frightening events described in the above two paragraphs! I once indulged in some cake that contained red frosting. Mama was glad that, after she partook of a piece, she had noted how red her teeth and gums were. Otherwise, on our trip to the park the next day, she would have thought I was hemorrhaging while performing some basic body functions.

In another slip, I had been sedated and had my teeth cleaned a week or two after Mama, Jessie, and I had spent an afternoon at Decker Lake. As I was a family member at the clinic, I got to wake up in the carpeted office instead of a cage. When Mama came back to check on me, her face paled and I thought she was going to faint. It wasn't because I had vomited a small volume, as that was to be expected; it was the content of the emesis that impacted her. In the center of the puddle were two affixed three-pronged fishhooks. Now Mama had seen the damage that can be caused by a dog swallowing a simple fishhook and how hard it was to remove. You can't just pull it out, you have to remove the barb first. She couldn't believe that I had actually been able to not only swallow but also regurgitate this hideous contraption with six hooks on it without causing damage to my intestinal tract. All she could figure was that I had swallowed a piece of food at the lake that contained the hooks (I did have a tendency to gulp my food), and because I always had a full tummy, there was enough padding to keep the fishhooks from implanting. She still has this sinister fishhook conglomeration in a jar for any disbelievers of this story to view!

Puppy Pal Pointer: Like children, puppy pals can and will get into anything that looks interesting or tasty and is accessible. Protect them from eating something harmful by securely putting such items out of reach of their mouths and keeping a watchful eye on them during outings.

RW

"Bug snacks are as much fun to make as they are to eat - but they are not a meal." - Michael Cader, *Meditations For Cats Who Do Too Much*, Penguin Books, 1993

"The diaper pail is not a cookie jar." - from *Things I Must Remember as a Dog* (provided by Jean Yates, a true critter lover and former student of Mama's)

If you change the antifreeze in your car or discover that some has leaked from your car, be sure to thoroughly clean it up and immediately remove it from your puppy pal's reach. This substance has an ethylene-glycol base, is attractive to animals due to a sweet taste, is highly toxic, and causes lethal kidney failure and metabolic acidosis (accumulation of acid in the blood and body tissues). A few licks (appoximately 1 to 2 ounces) can produce toxicity in a medium-sized dog. The brands that are propylene-glycol based instead of ethylene-glycol based are safer but still have the potential to cause complications.* If you suspect that puppy pals have ingested some antifreeze, waste no time in getting them to a veterinarian to begin treatment, and that means pronto!

* Joe Lamping, Flamingo Automotive, Austin, TX; John C. Haliburton, Texas A&M University, College Station, TX

I'd also like to add that I exhibited much more refined table manners than Jessie did. She was actually known to snatch food right from someone's plate while it was still on the table, although this practice diminished as she aged. As for me, I could be trusted. One joyous Christmas when Mama, Auntie Carol, and I were driving home to Illinois from Texas, we stopped for a visit at my Great-Aunt Carolyn and Great-Uncle Clif's house. (Regrettably, Cousin Kathy, a true critter lover and extraordinary being, was not there to celebrate the occasion with us and lavish me with her adoring attention.) They treated me like visiting royalty, including giving me carte blanche access to their soft, comfy sofa. Mama, traveling with the holiday spirit in mind, had brought a box of treats for me to give their Miniature Schnauzer, Gretel. We knew she would probably appreciate any edible Christmas gift because she had just recuperated from a bloating episode after eating an entire loaf of bread while left in the home temporarily unsupervised. As we were all adjourning for bed, Great-Uncle Clif set the box of treats on a table. His daughter, Lynn, tried to point out the folly in his action; she stated that the treats would be devoured during the night. When his response was that short-legged Gretel could not reach the box, Lynn looked directly at me, innocent me, and exclaimed, "No, but he can." With that, Great-Uncle Clif rose to my defense and explained that, unlike their own dog, I had good manners and could be trusted. (He did, on the sly, ask Mama if he was correct in that statement because he didn't want to be proven wrong in the morning, but I still feel he protected my honor!) Naturally, I proved to be the perfect guest and didn't consume the gift we had extended.

At another family gathering, I was making a debut performance with several Great-Aunts and a Great-Uncle. (All the relatives on the Wilson side of the family met me that day except Cousin Lindsay.) They were all having a high time enjoying appetizers and all the trimmings for sandwiches in Grandma and Grandpa's kitchen, at which time I was momentarily asked to wait on the outer side of the Dutch door. Mama, who could never eat anything without sharing some with me, started to take some ham slices to me. That's when Great-Aunt Nan whispered, "Don't worry, I've been slipping some to him." Well, this set forth an avalanche of confessions from Jane, Walt, Katy, and Ruth, plus Great-Grandma Wilson. Yep, they had all been sneaking slices of ham to me. It seems that, before my departure, I had just enough time to win them over with my engaging smile and whirling tail. My only complaint was that all that ham sure made me thirsty!

When Kim and Rick paid Mama a visit, they rearranged their tourist plans to include areas that were amenable to puppy pals. Jessie at the time was having a bout of kidney trouble and was housing an indwelling catheter in one of her front legs. As they had their own puppy pal, Alice, back home, they understood that Mama would only be able to relax and enjoy herself if she could keep an ever-watchful eye on her little girl. So they kindly ensured that every outing accommodated Jessie and her compromised condition.

Puppy Pal Pointer: Loving relatives and loyal friends will embrace and share in a person's devotion to a special puppy pal.

RW

"Money may buy you a fine dog, but only love can make it wag its tail." - Kinky Friedman (co-founder and bonefactor, along with Nancy Parker, of Utopia Animal Rescue Ranch, Medina, TX)

We could always tell when it was the weekend. There was a special feel in the air that told us Mama was not going to work that day. We would follow her in anticipation as she freshened up for the day, waiting for her to give the magical signal that it was time to load into the car for a ride to the lake or park. Mind you, if Mama ever started to act like she was diverging from this routine, we laid our remorseful eyes on her until her guilt couldn't handle it anymore and there was no way she could leave us behind. It was one way we kept the upper paw in these situations!

It should be noted that Mama derived as much pleasure as we did from these outings; just knowing she had made us infinitely happy gave her joy. She always carried dog treats in her pockets to help us maintain our strength and focus during rigorous hikes. Tasty treat rewards are grrrreat for any outing! Frequently after a Saturday trip to the lake, she would stop at an ice cream place and get a small scoop of ice cream for each of us. The standard joke from the ice cream salesman was that he'd ask us if we needed spoons. Yuk, yuk, yuk! We heard that one a million times. As I delicately licked my scoop, Ripple inhaled his. I often wondered if he got those headaches from eating something cold too fast. Then he'd sit and stare at Mama and me. Mama often remarked that people passing by the car probably thought she was cruel to eat ice cream on a hot summer day in front of her poor, starving, over-heated dog! On Sundays after our park trip, we would sit on the front porch with Mama while reading the newspaper and sharing a pack of powdered donuts or poppy seed muffins.

Weekends weren't the only times for outings. They say that every dog has its day; we ensured that we had seven special ones a week. Mama walked us every morning and every evening. She knew the first thing on the agenda when she got home from work was for us to go on our constitutional. Frequently we were joined by our best friends, Uncle David and T.C. There are not enough woofs to express how much we treasured our times spent with them.

Anytime Mama was running errands, we got to go along for the ride. Ripple faithfully sat in the front seat next to Mama, while I had the run of the back seat. One day a man crossing the road in front of our car at an intersection teasingly shouted to Mama, "Your boyfriend's a real dog!" We enjoyed our people-watching from the parking lot while Mama popped into a shop. Summers, however, were disappointing because our car trips were limited. Due to the heat, it was too dangerous to leave us in the car alone, even for just a few minutes. Never leave a puppy pal unattended in a car during hot weather; even with the windows cracked open, they could easily succumb to a deadly dose of heat stroke.

One time as a Christmas present, Mama took us some place different and special every day for a week, whether it was the lake, a park, or a friend's house. There's something fulfilling about a pair of pleasantly pooped pups! Although we still got packages to open, that was a present we all could enjoy. It was good exercise for all of us, plus a change of scenery always revives the spirit.

Puppy Pal Pointer: Puppy pals have routines that they anticipate. Learn from your puppy pal that exercise and fresh air should be part of your regular regimen.

JW

"I doubt whether the world holds for anyone a more soul-stirring surprise than the first adventure with ice cream" - Heywood Brown

"Dogs need to sniff the ground; it's how they keep abreast of current events. The ground is a giant dog newspaper, containing all kinds of late-breaking dog news items, which, if they are especially urgent, are often continued in the next yard." - Dave Barry

Ripple always loved a good party. As for me, I could do without them. I'd usually try to find a quiet room and hide when one was being held in my house. Ripple, on the other paw, was right in the middle of all activities. He'd be the first to arrive and the last to leave. Ripple was full of social graces. He was the official greeting committee for all our guests. I would rather nip a two-legged visitor on the hand or a four-legged visitor on the nose when they entered my domain than make them feel welcome!

Ripple especially enjoyed his own birthday parties. Nothing goes paw in paw with a party better than ice cream, cake, and homemade dog biscuits in cheese/garlic and chocolate flavors, plus cutout meat and cheese treats from Uncle David. Sometimes Ripple would get so excited that Mama would have to call a timeout from the festivities so he could relax. It's good to enjoy special moments and let puppy pals join in the fun; just be careful not to overdo it!

When our guest, T.C., would ignore his plate of cake and ice cream in true picky-Pekinese style, Ripple would politely hover over him and wait for him to abandon it. Then, being the good host that he was, he would clean the plate. There were always pawfuls of presents so everyone could join in the fun and open some of them. Ripple's birthday was the 4th of July, as was T.C.'s, so each year we got red, white, and blue bandanas and pinwheels. There were also bags and boxes of puppy pal treats and toys for all to share. As I was the most efficient at tearing gift wrap and opening presents, Ripple usually let me do so to speed up the process. He did supervise the whole event to make sure it went without a hitch and that I didn't eat all the loot!

Usually our parties included our best friend, T.C., and Uncle David. One year, though, other friends were invited. Given that parties were also in celebration of my half-birthday (based on my records, the birthday selected for me was December 22), invitations were sent with a note that no kids were allowed because one of the guests of honor did not care for children. After all, I should be able to attend my own party without the temptation for getting into trouble!

Ripple was a generous soul. He got excited about everyone's birthday. One night, Mama was up late making cupcakes for Auntie Carol's big day, including spelling out "Happy Birthday" on them. Ripple, bless his heart, stayed up all night guarding them in case they tried to escape. When Mama woke in the morning, she found him still sitting on the floor beneath the table that held them, ever staring upward. No letting sleeping dogs lie for him!

Puppy Pal Pointer: Celebrate your puppy pals' special days. Always remember that their birth is something to rejoice!

JW

"A dog is like an eternal Peter Pan, a child who never grows old and who therefore is always available to love and be loved." - Aaron Katcher

Ripple enjoys the creature comforts of a comforter and a satin pillowcase

Tater likes to curl his toes in a thick comforter and knead them to make biscuits

Sylvia seems to think a paper bag is comfy for a snooze, which makes little sense to dogs

Decker is content to be captain of a box boat; cats can relax in the strangest of places

All Wilson dogs, including Frisky, know the pleasure of opening presents (Uncle Randy watches in delight)

No box is too big for Jessie to tackle when she knows treats from Grandma and Grandpa wait within

Jessie puts her money where her mouth is as she demonstrates the fine art of opening a care package

After opening the outer box, Jessie knows treasure is lying beneath the pretty wrapping paper

Jessie reaps the rewards of opening her care package; she thinks the blanket from Auntie Carol is scrumptious

Time for Jessie to rest after a busy package-opening session; let sleeping dogs lie

Although Decker is a pro at opening gift bags, Mattie needs some prompting from Mama

Mattie gets the hang of opening gift bags after she discovers the catnip treats they hold

The paw is quicker than the eye; no bag is left unturned by our Christmas cat, Decker, who doesn't need catnip in order to act wacky

Mine, all mine! Decker loves Christmas and the toy joy it brings

Ripple and Jessie work out their differences and learn to share their treats; chew toys can help keep teeth clean and healthy

Ripple anxiously awaits treats from the Easter Bunny, so Jessie tries to fool him by dressing like the holiday visitor with the long ears

Auntie Carol and Ripple contemplate the chocolate under the snowman wrapper; take caution and remember that chocolate can be toxic to dogs

Abbey Wilson demonstrates the proper and polite method of begging; only give table scraps in moderation

Jessie Wilson demonstrates the pushy and rude method of begging (seen here with Auntie Carol and Ripple); make sure your puppy pal maintains a balanced diet of nutritious dog food

Frisky always shows his gentle nature, such as when he asks for a favor from Grandpa

Annie decides to take a new approach for begging from Grandpa (we thought only Ripple liked apples)

Ripple believes in good manners and proper puppy pal conduct at all times

Even in their early years, being around animals filled the Wilson family with glee (from left to right: Great-Aunt Nan, Grandpa, Great-Uncle Walt)

Due to her upbringing, it was natural for Great-Aunt Jane to treat puppy pals with tenderness

Alice had trained Kim and Rick to put her needs first; it was more common for them to bow before her

Auntie Carol commissioned her artistic neighbor, Melissa, to draw a portrait of a pair of perfectly precious pups, Ripple and Jessie

Aunt Mary's photography show, dedicated to Ripple, is a tribute to unusual pets and their people (Mama by pictures featuring her and handsome Ripple)

Opening night at the art gallery where faithful friends gather to admire Aunt Mary's photos of Ripple (from left to right: back - Gary, Susan, Jon, Vern, and Steve; front - Beth and Marilyn)

Kinky Friedman, co-founder of Utopia Animal Rescue Ranch, with Mama at the Texas Book Festival

Ripple dove through the car window to take the driver's seat at the start of a camping adventure with Mama and Uncle Bob; never leave a dog unattended in a car during hot weather

Jessie, Ripple, and T.C. always love a good birthday party; happy dogs are a joy to behold

Ripple and Jessie, ever the good sports, wear red, white, and blue bandanas in recognition of birthdays on the 4th of July

Ripple poses by the birthday cake in his honor; party favors in the form of homemade dog treats are healthy alternatives to cake

Be it birthday cupcakes or Halloween cookies, Ripple always keeps vigilant watch over the goodies

Understanding Your Puppy Pal

"If you can start the day without caffeine,
If you can get going without pep pills,
If you can always be cheerful, ignoring aches and pains,
If you can resist complaining and boring people with your troubles,
If you can eat the same food every day and be grateful for it,
If you can understand when your loved ones are too busy to give you any time,
If you can overlook it when those you love take it out on you when, through no fault of yours, something goes wrong,
If you can take criticism and blame without resentment,
If you can ignore a friend's limited education and never correct him/her,
If you can resist treating a rich friend better than a poor friend,
If you can face the world without lies and deceit,
If you can conquer tension without medical help,
If you can relax without liquor,
If you can sleep without the aid of drugs,
If you can honestly say that deep in your heart you have no prejudice against creed, color, religion, or politics,
Then, my friend, you are ALMOST as good as your dog."

Author Unknown
(but obviously a person who truly understands puppy pals)

One day Annie appeared to be looking for Grandpa. When Grandma said "Dad's by the tree," Annie immediately went to the front door. When Grandma added "No, he's out back," Annie changed directions and traipsed to the back door. Please don't tell me that we dogs don't understand what's being said to us! We know the voices and language of those who love us. True, sometimes our listening can be selective, like when Mama calls us to go for a constitutional when it's raining outside. Somehow, we just can't seem to hear her over the tap, tap, tap of the raindrops!

Grandpa always had the ability to form close relationships with puppy pals. When he worked nights at White Pines State Park during the summers, Frisky stayed alert and waited patiently for his return. Grandma could always tell when Grandpa's car was rounding the corner a block away because Frisky excitedly started to look out the window for his "Billy." Frisky also had a grasp for family interactions. He could interpret the tone of conversations and intuitively know what direction they were headed. When the occasional argument erupted, as will happen in even the soundest of households, he would hide beneath a bed until it subsided.

The ability to communicate with puppy pals must be hereditary. All Uncle Jeff had to do was give his wild call when he rounded the street corner while headed toward the house on foot, and Annie would go into a blaze of excitement in anticipation of his arrival.

Puppy Pal Pointer: Increase understanding between you and your puppy pal by increasing communication.

RW

"I think that one of the most important things people can do is talk to their animals. I'm convinced that they understand so much more than we realize." - Grandma

"It takes time and patience to develop a common language with your puppy pal, especially when working together on ventures such as house training." - Roxanne Matthys

A dog can tell the difference between the sounds of his master's footsteps and those of other people (courtesy of the 1999 *365 Dogs Calendar* by Workman Publishing).

For the most part, we Wilson dogs were adopted when we were nine months to a year of age. Understandably, we had some behavior slip-ups in our younger years that couldn't be avoided. Annie chewed a wood knob on an antique table and Auntie Carol's billfold (which technically was Auntie Carol's fault because she left it on her bed where a dog couldn't help but discover it). I probably had the biggest misadventure of all in the chewing department. During my very first week at Grandma and Grandpa's house, I was assigned to sleep in the family room. By the time Mama checked on me in the morning, I had chewed a major hole in the center cushion of their green couch. She looked at the bottom of the cavern I had created and noticed a rawhide chew toy. Bark about diggin' up bones! Was it my fault that, after I got started, I just couldn't stop? (I might add that Grandma and Grandpa demonstrated a true grandparent-type attitude toward the whole incident; they told Mama that at least it was their old couch, and it just must have been time to get rid of it.)

Jessie had some flare-ups as well. One night there was actually a snow flurry in Austin; such an event was indeed a rarity. When, independently, Mama and Auntie Carol returned home that particular evening, they each looked through the door window and thought it had snowed in the house via some unknown hole in the roof. Jessie had gotten them both with the old shred-the-stuffing-out-of-Auntie-Carol's-pillow-and-toss-it-all-over-the-living-room-floor gag! It wasn't so howling funny, though, when Jessie used to get into the garbage with similar gusto when Mama was away. I knew we were heading for big trouble and had no way of stopping her (how I wish I had a camera to prove my innocence in these mishaps!). She had the ability to listen to Mama's disciplinary voice about the disrupted garbage unheeded while I could only respond by looking remorseful and, therefore, ever so guilty. I'd follow Mama everywhere with a most pitiful look on my face until she gave me the hug of total forgiveness. One good thing was that Mama only scolded us verbally; she never roasted our rumps with her hands. She knew we could understand the inflection of her voice and that physical reprimand was not necessary. It's tough having a kid sister, but my spirits were kept unwaveringly high with the thought that, like me, she would grow up to be perfect.

There were pups who tried to mimic Jessie's unruly behavior. Cousin Abbey, while staying overnight at Grandma's house, had her own slumber party and shredded the pillows. On the other paw, Grandma had the audacity to leave her unattended in an unfamiliar abode! So, in reality, who was truly at fault?

Puppy Pal Pointer: Your puppy pals will grow up all too fast; be understanding when they have a behavior set back (haven't we all?) and regress into puppyhood. Your patience will be amply rewarded.

RW

"A dog is the only thing on earth that loves you more than he loves himself." - Josh Billings

While we are on the topic of behavior gone astray, I'd like to mention how stressful it has been for me, such a perfect pup, to live with those less likely to practice restraint. Let me present a few cases in point.

One day Jessie and I were both in the proverbial dog house when the trash can in the kitchen was disrupted. As usual, I took my reprimand to heart while Jessie didn't understand what all the fuss was about and, therefore, ignored it. Mama never stayed upset with us for long, just enough to set a few behavior boundaries for us, so it was off to Bastrop State Park with Auntie Carol, Uncle Bob, and Uncle David by the following day. As we were frolicking through the pine needles, a strange yellow flag was seen wafting from

Jessie's rump as she sped past us to catch the next scent of interest. Upon closer examination, the tattle*tail* material was determined to be part of the yellow wrapper from the chicken we all had feasted upon just a few days prior; the wrapper was last seen when it was laid to rest in the trash. There was no denying it now; she was guilty, and I was reprieved!

Then there was the time Mama was working at the clinic on a Saturday morning. Aunt Joyce had brought everyone a glazed doughnut to start their busy day on a sweet note. Mama had to set her taste treat down in order to wait on a customer. When she returned to her napkin, it was empty and the doughnut was gone without a trace! She began blaming her co-worker, Benny, for the dastardly deed while he expounded on his innocence. Then she noticed Bubbles, an over-stuffed black cat who dwelled at the clinic, taking in the doughnut drama with disbelief at Benny's presumed activities. Unfortunately for Bubbles, he had forgotten to use a napkin and had incriminating glazed sugar encircling his lips!

Last, but definitely not least, is the story of our cat cousins, Ketra and Cato. In our younger days, Uncle Jeff would pop over to Texas and stay with us for a month or so at a time. We puppies loved for him to visit, and we showed him the respect he deserved and followed his every lead. However, Ketra and Cato, Auntie Carol's cataclysmic duo, were not so astute in their appreciation of Uncle Jeff's wonderfulness. Poor Uncle Jeff suddenly started noticing an aroma to his clothes, shoes, and backpack. Our keen noses had no doubt as to the source of this offensive odor; it was cat urine! No matter how many times Uncle Jeff washed his clothes and no matter where he tried to hang them or hide them, they'd be hit again with the same offensive discharge. All we could figure was that the time Uncle Jeff spent in the woods had made his apparel particularly enticing. As Ketra was a female cat, her name was cleared and Cato, even though he was neutered, was put at the top of the spraying suspect list. We chastised him every time he neared an item of Uncle Jeff's. After all, these careless acts had his pawprints all over them, or so we thought. Then, on his last night with us, Uncle Jeff was lying on the couch with his head near Auntie Carol's glass-door bookcase. His pack was sitting near it too. To our amazement,

Ketra edged her hind end up to the bookcase, sprayed a strong, fierce stream, and hightailed it out of the room! Much to Cato's good fortune, she just couldn't keep a secret and hold out for one more day, so the truth set him free. Through the years, Mama learned that female cats could spray with as much ferocity as a neutered male, but their spray couldn't match the potent aroma as that of an intact male.

Puppy Pal Pointer: In the world of puppy pals and kit-kats, things aren't always the way they appear to be. Don't make hasty judgments!

RW

"Cat's Motto: No matter what you've done wrong, always try to make it look like the dog did it." - Author Unknown

"I have studied many philosophers and many cats. The wisdom of cats is infinitely superior." - Hippolyte Tain

"To err is human, to forgive canine." - Author Unknown

Treats can go a long way toward modifying behavior, which is evidenced in the infamous true tale of Frisky Wilson. This pup was so smart that he would steal any item that his family members left out, including such things as pencils, troll dolls, rat fink rings, miniature rubber animals called itsy-bitsies, jewelry, pocket mirrors, and keys. You name it, he stole it. Even an innocent porcelain sheep from the Christmas manger scene was fair game. He would gingerly stand on his hind legs, put his front paws on the edges of dressers and tables, and slowly cruise the surface until he found an item within reach that could fit in his mouth. He was so stealth in this endeavor that he rarely got caught red-pawed. Then he was off to hide just out of arm's reach behind the old-fashioned bathtub, which was perched on short, ornate legs. The only way he would surrender his prize was in a trade for a cookie. And I mean a real cookie, as in peanut butter, chocolate chip, or Oreo!* Now I had the ability to pick the word "cookie" out of any conversation to the extent that family members spelled the word when I was in their midst so they wouldn't get me excited, but even I didn't work the system like this pup! If the household was fresh out of cookies, someone would have to rattle the cookie jar lid before offering him a different taste treat. That pup had initiative and was definitely one sharp cookie himself!

Frisky would wait for Grandpa to take a coffee break from grading papers; then he'd patrol the table's edge on tippaws for the ever present red pen. I suspect that sometimes Grandpa purposely left it there just to brighten Frisky's evening and make his vigil worthwhile. When Grandpa's colleague and close friend, Mr. Harland, was visiting the house one day, this brazen pup gently clipped his eyeglasses from his hand and didn't even put a single scratch on them. During another social visit, he stole none other than Reverend Holler's hat right out of his hand and was off to his hide out. Saints be praised! To top it off, he was rewarded with a C-O-O-K-I-E for his cocky behavior. My hero!

Treats were offered for a different reason in Jessie's case. She had developed a reputation of being a nipster, which earned her the fear of friends and family. Although she was somewhat flirtatious to male dogs, she hated all female dogs. When we would take our late afternoon walks down the various alleys, Jessie was always picking fights through fences with the back-street girls, Uhla and Ginger, and they definitely responded in kind. Why, she even got in a fight with my good pal, sweet little Annie, during her first visit to Grandma and Grandpa's house. What a way to make a memorable impression!

An even worse impact was made when she nipped Grandma the first time she met her. What a faux pas! You can imagine our horror, as all dogs and cats loved Grandma! We tried to rationalize that, after the long trip from Texas to Illinois, Jessie found herself in a strange house with a strange woman trying to steal Mama's coat (Grandma was putting it in the closet) and lost control.

It was several years later by the time we figured out that Jessie could be bought. When Mama wanted to let a friend, Laura, stay overnight at her house, they had to get permission from Jessie because she had sneered at Mama's friend in the past. Laura sat on the couch with a box of Snausages.** With ample offerings of the luscious treat, she was able to win Jessie's affections. Mama had Grandma try the same technique; to everyone's delight, it worked. Grandma and Jessie became close friends. Jessie even let Grandma sleep in her bed when Grandma visited Texas. Every morning she would patter into her room where Grandma was staying and stare at her as if to say, "This is my room, Grandma! When are you getting up and getting out?" As a side note, I also can attest to the power of Snausages. When we would be on a lengthy hike and I wanted to stop before reaching our special place at Decker Lake, Mama would tempt me with Snausages like a bird following a trail of bread crumbs; a Snausage picnic was always part of our outings.

When Aunt Janet came to visit us, her dad had warned her to "be careful around the little brown dog." OK, so Jessie did make her most horrible snarling face at him when we were visiting him and his wife while en route from Texas to Illinois. Still, you've got to give puppy pals a chance to prove they can change (or can be bribed!). Naturally, Aunt Janet and I immediately became a close item, but a few treats and some coaxing later, she and Jessie were also on good terms.

Our Aunt Mary G. once told us that her neighbor's kids used to taunt her larger-than-life German Shepherd, Shea, because he barked at them. It accelerated to where the kids were throwing rocks at Shea over the fence. She finally gave them a bag of dog treats and asked them to throw those instead. Using this technique, an understanding was magically formed between Shea and the kids.

We put this theory to work during our neighborhood walks with Uncle David and T.C. We would stroll down the alley and visit with a wide variety of dogs who were separated from us by their back-yard fences. Snuff, a small, black Cocker mix, and Chuy, a somewhat goofy, fawn-colored Doberman pup, were easily succumbed by our charms. Chuy's big "brother," a sizeable black and tan Doberman, was a more formidable encounter. His name was Satan or some such demonic sounding name, and he acted the part. Mama was a little timid when we would pass by his turf even though he was on the opposite side of a fence. Then one day before we headed on our neighborhood tour, she stuffed her pockets with Snausages and Milk-Bones.*** As soon as she offered one to this tough pup, he mellowed and we all became fast friends. She shared some of the tasty treats with Snuff and Chuy also (just a few, though, because she didn't want to give them any type or amount of food that their owners wouldn't want them to have). After all, good behavior needs to be rewarded too. That became our evening ritual much to the delight of our canine community.

Puppy Pal Pointer: Pawsitively speaking, you can win more puppy pal friendships with treats than with teasing or torment. To improve relations with a puppy pal or to get better behavioral results, use treats and kindness, not teasing, cruelty, or physical force.

RW

"Dogs have given us their absolute all. We are the center of their universe. We are the focus of their love and faith and trust. They serve us in return for scraps. It is without a doubt the best deal man has ever made." - Roger Caras

"We give dogs time we can spare, space we can spare, and love we can spare. And in return, dogs give us their all. It's the best deal man has ever made." - M. Facklan

Dogs that are fear biters will bite when they are scared. They may have their ears and tails down and lean away from you when you approach them. If you get too close to them, they may snap at you. To calm fear biters, move slowly, talk in a soft voice, squat down on one knee and turn sideways (to appear less threatening), pat your thigh and quietly call to them, touch them under their chins (not on the top of their heads), and handle them gently to calm them. (Excerpts taken from the Texas Department of Health, Zoonosis Control Division's *Animal Control Officer Training Manual*.)

* Oreo - a product of Nabisco, East Hanover, NJ 07936
** Snausages - a product of Heinz Pet Products, Newport, KY 41071

*** Milk-Bones - a product of Nabisco, East Hanover, NJ 07936

Summer has its own set of safety scenarios. There was the first-trip-to-the-ocean legend in which Auntie Carol, Mama, and I packed up the car and drove to the Texas Coast for fun, sun, rest, and relaxation. When we hit the beach, I wisely refused to set a paw in the nasty salt water. Instead, I amused myself with burying treats in the sand and lying on the beach blanket watching all the girls go by. (Why not? They all stopped to admire me and thought I was pretty cute!). In the meantime, Auntie Carol and Mama were having a high time jumping in waves near the shore. Being ocean novices, they didn't realize that the undertow had gradually taken them out to sea. Not having astute powers of observation like we puppy pals, there was a time lag before they noticed how much they had drifted. They then struggled to return to shore. Before long, they both were fairly certain that they were going to drown. Finally, they quit fighting the undertow and started to ride the pounding waves, which eventually returned them to me. Mama then professed that all she had on her mind while in the process of being engulfed by the ocean was that I would be patiently waiting for their return to no avail, all alone and confused as to where they were and why they had left me by myself. When will they ever learn to follow their puppy pal's good sense? I couldn't quite put my paw on it, but for some reason I knew that salt water was trouble from the start.

We used to go on outings to various lakes around Austin fairly frequently during the dog days of summer. Mama would feign that she needed to be rescued in order to draw us into the water. We would humor her to an extent. We dog paddled fairly close to her and then did a semicircle turn in front of her in order to head back to the shore. One day Jessie actually passed right by Mama (not really interested in saving her at all!) and was headed for a woman on a bright orange float. As she had been known, on occasion, to roll her upper lip and "smile" at people, Mama and Auntie Carol were frantically calling her back to them. They didn't want an unpleasant incident during our outing; after all, one chomp from Jessie into that float and that woman would have been on a sinking ship! This became known as our raft patrol's "shark-in-the-water" episode.

During another lake outing, we were peacefully sunning on some rocky cliffs with Mama, Auntie Carol, and Uncle Bob. A couple appeared with two young puppies who were eager to play. These folks got in the water and called their puppies to them somewhat like Mama did with us. However, because the puppies hesitated before jumping into the water, when they finally got to their owners, these poor youngsters were hit and held under water. How pupposterous! When Uncle Bob asked the people to stop this brutish practice, they started yelling to him about not wanting wimpy dogs like he had. (Yes, they meant Jessie and me! How more unbelievable can this story get? They obviously didn't know that Jessie was proud of her title of being "the most horrible.") This was absolutely abusive behavior. No wonder their puppies hesitated and didn't want to swim toward them; after all, where's the trust? Trips to the lake should be designed to make tail-wagging memories, not fearful ones. Mama felt it was like taking a kid to a carnival expecting a fun-filled time and then hitting and yelling at him instead. The only redeeming part of this story was that, quite unexpectedly a few weeks later, these same folks brought their puppies to a clinic where Mama worked. As the manner in which they screamed their puppies' names was still ringing in her ears, she recognized them immediately and, subsequently, reported them to the Humane Society.

On a side note, lawn chairs can pose a summer hazard. On a trip to the lake that Mama took with her friends, Esther accompanied them. She was a very petite Whippet who could fit right under a lawn chair. You guessed it! The chair, along with the person it contained, collapsed right on this skinny mini-package of a dog. Miraculously, no damage was done. Mama always remembered this scene when she stretched out in a lawn chair in our back yard. She made sure the legs were locked in place, and she ever so gingerly would reposition herself when need be because our kitties loved to take turns lying underneath the chair and playing with her, especially when she teasingly taunted them with long blades of grass. Even though Mama tried to be careful, there were some close-call mishaps. Fortunately, those kitties are fast on their paws when somebody more than 10 times their size is about to land on them! As for me, I stayed away from these sun-drenched activities and enjoyed relaxing inside with a fan blowing on me. I always was considered the wise one of the group!

Puppy Pal Pointer: Make outings during the dog days of summer safe and fun for your puppy pals. Also remember that negative treatment is not the best way to get a positive response from your puppy pals.

RW

"In the whole history of the world there is but one thing that money cannot buy - to wit, the wag of a dog's tail." - Henry Wheeler Shaw

"George Attla, a top racer of sled dogs in the 1960s, said that you could train a dog with fear or with love. Those trained with fear would always weigh the pain of performance with the pain of the whip. Those trained with love would give you everything they had." - Uncle Jeff

Neither Ripple nor I cared for outings in the rain, but Ripple developed avoidance of them into a masterpiece. Just because it was raining cats and dogs didn't mean we wanted to join them! If it was raining early in the morning, he would give the impression of being in a deep, comfortable sleep. He displayed to Mama that he was just too tired to go outside and that she should check with him later. When Mama finally roused him, she knew she would have to do more than release him in the fenced yard for him to perform essential duties because he would stay plastered to the back door. She had to put on her raincoat and head for the fence gate in order to walk us down the alley. By the time she reached the gate, she would notice she was alone. Ripple and I would be watching from the back porch and wishing her bon voyage on her stroll!

It took Mama awhile to figure out that Ripple was afraid of firecrackers and thunder. When Mama and Ripple first joined forces, he never seemed to flinch at these noises from the outside world. Then one 4th of July, she came home to find us both huddled behind a living room chair. She tried to explain to us that people were just celebrating Ripple's birthday by exploding firecrackers (after all, with the 4th of July being his birthday, he was a Yankee Doodle Dog), but we weren't buying her sale. By the next year, we were shaking in our paws from the distant cannon balls suddenly being fired over Town Lake. We needed to have Mama sit close to us to still our fears, and Ripple insisted that she maintain hand contact with his body. If she ever removed her hand, he would plop his paw on her arm to remind her of his need and of her duty!

It didn't take long before Ripple's fear of fireworks transferred to a fear of thunder. He was so sensitive about it that he would start pacing about half an hour before the oncoming storm was evident to anyone else. We pups are really attuned to changes in barometric pressure. Mama was very understanding of it because she used to know owners who had to buy pet-approved sedatives from the clinic for their dogs during storms or fireworks lest they seizure. Even worse, they could panic, tear a hole in a screen door or window, and disappear into the night. There are just some things you can't rationalize to us puppies, such as loud, unexpected noises. She even made an arrangement with Uncle David so he would stay with us during a storm when she was working the evening shift at the clinic. It was awhile before they compared notes and found that Ripple displayed a brave front for Uncle David and never once showed his fear of thunder while he was at the house!

Annie, too, was afraid of thunder. During one rain of terror, she was timidly huddled on the couch near Mama. In a nearby cage, Cassidy,* their tiny gerbil, was bravely running in his wheel undaunted by the noise being generated from the sky. Grandpa, who was viewing this scene, told Cassidy, "You really know how to hurt a guy!" Even a little gerbil displayed more bravery than she did. Poor little scaredy-dog Annie! I guess I shouldn't have been so mean and gotten into a fight with her when we first met. (However, it still has not been proven who actually started that fight; I'm not admitting to any ill conduct on my part, and I wash my paws of the whole affair.)

One other noisemaker who was a formidable foe for Ripple was the vicious vacuum cleaner. You can imagine his fear when this roaring beast would enter the safe sanctuary of his home. During one visit to Grandma and Grandpa's house, Mama, Auntie Carol, and Grandma decided to go shopping. They left Ripple pleased as punch to be spending a relaxing afternoon with his cherished grandpa; he was probably looking forward to the two of them taking a nice, leisurely nap together. When Mama called to check in on Ripple, Grandpa reported that all was well and then happened to mention, "He sure doesn't like the vacuum cleaner." Horror of all horrors for Ripple, his very own grandpa (aka Mr. Clean) had decided to take the noisy beast for a stroll over the carpet! As soon as Grandpa learned of Ripple's fears, he desisted and returned the beast to its closet lair. In his usual style, Ripple immediately forgave his grandpa for his crazed act of cleanliness.

Puppy Pal Pointer: Be understanding and compassionate about your puppy pals' fears; after all, they are the ones who not only calm your fears, but accept you in spite of them.

JW

"My dog does have his failings, of course. He's afraid of firecrackers and hides in the clothes closet whenever we run the vacuum cleaner; but, unlike me, he's not afraid of what other people think of him or anxious about his public image." - Gary Kowalski, *The Souls of Animals*

"Run - don't walk - at the nearest hint of a vacuum cleaner." - Michael Cader, *Meditations For Cats Who Do Too Much*, Penguin Books, 1993

"Thunder - this is a signal that the world is coming to an end. Humans remain amazingly calm during thunderstorms, so it is necessary to warn them of the danger by trembling uncontrollably, panting, rolling your eyes wildly, and following at their heels." - Doggy Dictionary

* Cassidy was named after *Cassidy* (by Weir and Barlow), a song on Bob Weir's album, *Ace* (Warner Bros. Records, Inc., 1972)

I was a pretty passive pup for the most part. I tolerated the invasion of my home by Jessie and a cluster of cats, plus any orphaned squirrel babies or kittens to which Mama was tending. Just as during the Depression era when hobos would leave a mark of a smiling cat on a kindhearted woman's house so other drifters would know it was a good place to get a handout, I fervently believe that there were little signs at animal eye level posted around our home letting critters know that this was a place where they could rest their weary souls and get a good meal. Every so often, I had to put my paw down when these intruders got carried away with the share-and-share-alike scheme. If I was approached while chewing on a meaty bone fresh from a restaurant doggy bag or a beef-basted chew stick fresh from the grocery bag, I made my "Mr. Ugly" face at anyone who treaded in my territory. I simply lifted my entire upper lip until it made my nose wrinkle; no barks were even necessary to convey the "beat it, kid, I'm busy" message!

We puppy pals can read body language and facial expressions of people. We can tell when folks are glad, sad, or mad as well as tense or sick. In doing so, we know how to best support and comfort our people pals. By the same token, we have body language and facial expressions of our own that tell a story of what we are feeling. I've been told that, when I get upset, I puff my cheeks. I had nothing on Jessie. I verbalized with my face; she threw her whole body into the message she wanted to convey and made body language into an art. When she was being disciplined with even a slightly raised voice, she would throw the side of her body to the ground and raise the set of upper legs in what Mama and Auntie Carol cited as an "emergency belly rub." They would stop in mid-sentence, melt to their knees, and shower her belly with affectionate rubs. If she was particularly nervous over a situation, she'd form a big yawn and let out an impressive squeaky noise.

When Jessie first came to us, her left front leg was broken. Years after it was healed, she would lift it whenever she anticipated any chance of getting in trouble, such as after a trash can raid. It was as if she were saying, "Remember me? I'm the one with the injured leg." She was akin to the character portrayed by Danny Kaye in Irving Berlin's *White Christmas*; when he wanted something, he would rub his arm to remind Bing Crosby that he had injured it while saving Bing's life. Who could resist this pity-evoking routine? It surely wasn't Mama, Auntie Carol, or Bing!

Puppy Pal Pointer: Puppy pals use body language; take time to learn how to interpret it so you develop a better understanding of each other. If you learn to read it right, it can tell you if puppy pals are happy, sad, upset, or sick.

RW

"A dog can express more with his tail in minutes than his owner can express with his tongue in hours." - Anonymous

"Dogs laugh, but they laugh with their tails." - Max Eastman

Submissive dogs may whine and whimper, tuck their tails between their legs, hold their ears down, roll on their sides or backs, and/or urinate when touched. Aggressive dogs may growl, have raised hair on their necks and backs (hackles), curl their lips in a snarl, move their tails from side to side (flagging), stand erect, look directly at a person, flatten their ears against their heads, tuck their tails between their legs, and/or bare their teeth. If you encounter a dog that appears to be aggressive, do not move quickly or make any sudden movements, do not try to run from the dog, and do not stare into the dog's eyes (this can be threatening to the dog). (Excerpts taken from the Texas Department of Health, Zoonosis Control Division's *Animal Control Officer Training Manual*.)

Puppy pals have their own pals. Our Auntie Carol used to make us fancy sock puppets in all different shapes and forms, such as octopi, bunnies, and ponies. Ripple's first favorite puppet was a tan bunny. One time Mama heard him knock on the door to come inside just moments after he had gone outside. When she opened the door, he ran to the bedroom, grabbed his bunny puppet, and asked to go outside again. He wanted his favorite toy with him during playtime! He even insisted on taking it along during our walks; Mama, however, would be the one to carry it home because his mouth eventually would tire of it. One time, in a fit of passion, I disassembled one of the puppets of which Ripple was particularly fond. I had to mail its now multiple parts to Auntie Carol for her to weave her magic and repair it before Ripple noticed it was missing in action!

As for me, I had Pengui, a plush, light blue and white penguin who squeaked when I nibbled into his belly. Mama had to perform surgery and suture Pengui a few times so I could enjoy him for many additional years. There was something about squeaky toys that made me nibble them with extra fervor; I guess it was the lifelike sound they made when I was chewing on them that stirred my hunter instincts. Grandma and Grandpa had also sent me some neat toys, including Pink Bunny, who came with a heart-shaped tag with the phrase "Just a reminder, somebody loves you a lot," which was the truth!

Mama could always tell when our neighbors, Uncle David or Barb, were out and about. Ripple's bark would sound happier and more excited than usual. His tail's wag-o-meter would also be going off the chart. Although Ripple was everyone's best friend, he certainly had folks he rated extra high on his list. If Ripple had worn a shirt, you would have found his heart on its sleeve for all to see.

Puppy Pal Pointer: Puppy pals, like you, have best friends, special relationships, and favorite possessions that they treasure. Follow your puppy pal's lead; don't be afraid to show your happiness and wag your tail in public.

JW

"The reason a dog has so many friends is that he wags his tail instead of his tongue." - Anonymous

"It's true, dogs and cats don't feel emotions like we feel them, but that doesn't mean they don't feel them." - Dr. Allen Schoen, *How the Remarkable Bond Between Humans & Animals Can Change the Way We Live: Kindred Spirits*, Broadway Books

"Dogs greet us with so much unbridled energy. Shouldn't we show them the same level of enthusiasm when they welcome us at the front door?" – Uncle Randy

We could only speculate on Ripple's intense reaction to the mailperson. He would lie in wait for hours with his chin resting on the back of the couch gazing out the window until he spied one of them approaching the walk. Then the howls of alert sounded even when it was Lupe, our friendly, faithful mailman for many years. It was always enough to encourage me to come running and chime in with the commotion. Our Uncle Randy developed the theory that we dogs got upset at our mailpersons because every day they come to the front door, but no one seems to trust them enough to let them enter the house. Then these mailpersons leave and try, to no avail, to enter the neighbors' houses. This happened day after day. No wonder we viewed them as intruders! Ripple was so in tune to this phenomenon that once, after covering many miles of a journey from Texas to Illinois, we drove past a parked mail truck on a busy city street. Ripple was not fooled; he started barking voraciously at the suspicious vehicle.

Some confusion did enter his mind on this issue once. An old friend and neighbor of ours, Megan, had become a mailperson and donned the mystery uniform. One day Mama let Megan in the house for a drink of water while she was on her route. Ripple lunged at her, paused when he realized who it was, and then wagged his tail. He almost put his paw in his mouth that time! He just couldn't figure out how he was supposed to react. As always, Ripple's overwhelmingly kind and accepting side was victorious; he accepted her into our home with open paws.

Puppy Pal Pointer: Even puppies sometimes judge a person by the cover they wear, but their minds are always kept open to a change in perception. That's another lesson you can learn from puppy pals.

JW

"A man's best friend is his dog." - Lord Byron

"Properly trained, a man can be dog's best friend." - Cory Ford

Ripple never met a dog he didn't like. When he was titled "Everyone's Best Friend," everyone was included be they two-, three-, or four-legged in nature. Once, almost beyond my comprehension, there was a dog that didn't seem to care for him. We were walking down a neighborhood alley with Mama when a Pit Bull that was tied to a large rock jumped his fence, rock and all, and landed between Mama and Ripple. Mama tried to coax Ripple past the uncouth beast while she kept tight reins on me. The aggressor was slowed by the rock he was dragging, but Ripple sensed the animosity and timidly wagged his tail at him. As Ripple finally tried to pass him, the mad dog lunged for his throat; Mama could later feel the saliva drops that he left on Ripple's neck! Mama screamed at the dog and its owners who were standing like slack-jawed mutants in their back yard observing the whole transaction. Go figure, you just can't reason with some animals. Maybe they don't know better because they are just taking after their obtuse owners.

Speaking of Pit Bulls, I also had a harrowing experience with one. When I was almost 16, Mama and I were peacefully and very slowly strolling in the park early on a Sunday morning. Suddenly, we heard a woman yelling the name "Bob." Mama turned to see a Pit Bull barreling toward me, and she could tell by his determination that he wasn't paying us a friendly call. She pulled me forward as he dived and went to chomp on me. Woof! Mama thought that it would be safer for me to be bit on my back end than in the throat. When the woman finally captured Bob, she admitted that she knew of his personality deficit and had brought him to the park to release him and try to teach him voice commands. Needless to say, Mama let her have some voice commands of her own! She pointed out that the park, where other animals and children were playing, was no place to teach voice commands to a mean-spirited dog. She also informed the woman that a bite on an older dog, especially near the kidneys as in my case, could set off a series of physical problems that could cost an animal its life. Not only did this woman and Bob get an earful, but all the inhabitants of the entire park heard this Sunday morning sermon!

Now I'm not trying to stereotype and present a negative portrait of any one breed, but I have heard yet another disconcerting story involving Pit Bulls. In the episode faced by Mama's friend, Jan, and Koontz, her small, light brown, mixed-breed dog, there were two Pit Bulls. Jan and Koontz were serenely conducting their Sunday afternoon gardening chores in the safety and privacy of their fenced yard. In the yard next door, they could hear the neighbor's two Pit Bulls exercising their usual barking ritual. As Jan was moving a sprinkler, she heard a different level of commotion and turned to see the Pit Bulls in her yard in the process of tearing Koontz to shreds! Somehow they had squeezed through an opening in the fence. It was horrible! They were tossing Koontz about like a rag doll, and Jan could see they had murder in their eyes. She hit them with the hose and her shoe, but her efforts were to no avail. Another neighbor heard the screams and rushed to their aid. It took several whacks with an axe handle before these savages even realized they were being hit and finally dropped Koontz during a retreat. As much as I like to terrorize kitty cats, I'd never treat one that drastically, let alone do something so dreadful to one of my own species. The high note on which I can end this tale is that, after extensive surgery, Koontz survived and continued to live the good life with Jan.

Still, you don't want to judge a dog by his breed. When Mama heard that Gary G. had adopted Dusty, a puppy who strongly resembled a Rottweiler, a warning chill ran up and down her back. Although she respected him for adopting a puppy who was basically being given away at the side of a country road and was in need of a home, a breed that was no fun to treat at the clinic was the Rottweiler. One of the nicer Rottweilers who was a patient at the clinic showed his savage side at home. He and his Rottweiler sibling were found chewing on opposite ends of a Dachshund who shared the same house with them. Guess they thought they were at a picnic and he was the obligatory wiener. All they needed was some sauerkraut to match their dispositions. They were yet more examples of followers of the dog-eat-dog dogma! Another time a Rottweiler who was sedated to have his teeth cleaned did a real "Cujo" on Aunt Joyce. As she went to get the dozing dog out of his cage, he unexpectedly jolted awake, lunged at her, and knocked her to the floor. The only thing keeping his mouth from eating her face was the strength in her arms holding him a foot away. Amazingly, he soon nodded out again, and Aunt Joyce was unscathed. The other happy ending was to the Gary G. and Dusty story, as she matured into a sweetheart of a dog.

Puppy Pal Pointer: Train your puppy pals to get along with other animals. If this is impossible, be responsible and do not expose other animals or children to their aggression.

JW

According to dogma, "Avoid biting when a simple growl will do."

For one all too brief time in our lives, Mama and I lived together with Auntie Carol and her first cat, Stella Blue (so named because this quiet, sleek, black stray suddenly leaped up and playfully nipped at Auntie Carol's shoulder as she was singing the Grateful Dead's *Stella Blue* while bathing in the tub). For the most part, we tolerated each other and even took somewhat of an interest in each other's activities.

We always enjoyed going on an outing and getting exercise, which was good for all of us as well as being a pleasant family activity. When Auntie Carol walked me, Stella Blue would join us. She was always just a few aloof paces back, acting as if she was out for a walk by herself and happened to be going that way anyway; it had nothing at all to do with us. When Auntie Carol spied a loose dog, she would say "Dog, Stella, dog," and Stella would climb a tree or hide until danger passed. Then she'd join us down the street.

When Mama walked me, Stella occasionally hid in some bushes in the path ahead and jumped out with paws raised to scare us. If Mama spotted her before Stella had a chance to spring, she'd say very loudly, "Oh, helloooo, Stella," and Stella would slowly stretch out of the bushes and lick herself like she really wasn't hiding after all and didn't know what Mama meant by that tone in her voice.

Puppy Pal Pointer: Every day is full of excitement and adventure if you just know where to look!

RW

"Life's full of surprises. Enjoy!" - Auntie Carol

"There are many intelligent species in the universe. They are all owned by cats." - Author Unknown

"Thousands of years ago, cats were worshiped as gods. Cats have never forgotten this." - Author Unknown

On our daily constitutionals, we would see Lance, an untidy, edgy Airedale Terrier, who was always on a chain in his back yard. He appeared to be slightly on the crazed side and barked ferociously at passersby. He eventually got used to us and let us continue our journey without a single "Woof!" Still, his owners warned us to never approach him. One day we noticed Lance lying in the dirt; this was not unusual except for the small, warm form curled up next to him. Our very own Tater-Bug was hanging out with Lance and providing him with some much needed companionship. Tater could conquer the toughest of souls with his cool cattitude.

Jessie was very aggressive toward cats. While on otherwise peaceful walks, Jessie had the tendency to dive at any strange cat that dared to be lurking in her alley. You could tell she would just love to catch and treat the critter like one of her squeaky toys; good thing for those kitties that Jessie was always on a leash. The cat, now running from what was thought to be a secure hiding place, always created quite a ruckus. One day when we were on the alley side of our gate after a walk, Jessie dove at a cat lying in the nearby shrubs. Mama was so sure it was our very own Mattie Lou that she started saying "Get the kitty, Jessie, get the kitty" in her usual playful way. Suddenly, it dawned on her that the cat not only was not moving, it wasn't even Mattie! The poor thing had a fractured back; we speculated that she got hit by a car and had bravely pulled herself away from the nearby road. Unfortunately, after a month of treating Mattie-Look-Alike-Kitty at the clinic, she had to be euthanized. Mama gave her a final home and resting place.

When a new cat was introduced into our household Mama would simply tell Jessie "This is one of your cats," and she would amazingly accept them. Although Jessie learned to like her cats and the multiple cats at the animal clinic (namely Sheba, Bubbles, Sam, Brillo, Roger, Sarah, and Frankie), she still found it hard to not react aggressively to a new set of kitty whiskers while on a walk.

There have been dogs of our acquaintance who had a passionate dislike of cats. Our puppyhood friends, Tasha and Buffy, are prime examples. One week, Mama was puppy-sitting these two little brown dogs. Her first clue that trouble was brewing was when the pipes underneath the house started to shake and quake. She discovered that the source of this commotion was Tasha chasing Country Kitty under the house a little too assertively. Later that day, Mama was talking to a neighbor by the fence. In a surreal moment, a stray kitten who appeared from nowhere jumped toward them and landed in our yard! Without hesitation, Tasha and Buffy were attacking it. Jessie was egging them on, but I viewed the whole situation at a distance and with disdain. Mama was desperately trying to lift the kitten over the fence, but the jaws of life kept pulling his small body downward. Finally, the tiny soul escaped, climbed a nearby tree, and collapsed on a branch. Mama was worried that he would go into shock after such trauma, but she couldn't even reach him with a ladder. As she was trying to coax him down the tree with a can of cat food, Tater came along and surveyed the predicament. He then slowly climbed the tree paw by paw in telephone-repairperson style and rescued the kitten! The kitten was dubbed "Tater's Tot," and the story had a happy ending. As a side note, when Tasha matured, she mellowed and even allowed a roaming cat to take up residence in her yard. As unbelievable as this may seem, we just figured she had tired of the senseless chase.

Given that well-earned lesson, Mama now believed people when they said their puppy pals did not like cats. She used to think that people just didn't give puppy pals the necessary time, under supervision, to adjust to any newcomer critters in their abodes. Needless to say, future puppy-sitting endeavors of Tasha and Buffy entailed Mama going to their house where they were content and sans cats in their own back yard.

That's also why friends' otherwise happy-go-lucky, fun-filled pups never got to come to our house to play if they couldn't be trusted around cats. Mama never wanted to endure such a close call ever again, and she didn't want any of our kit-kat club members to have to either. Even with trying to take precautions, Mama sadly endured an even worse dog attack on one of her cats some years later. Sweet-natured Licorice was peacefully snoozing by the street curb when he was attacked by a 110-pound German Shepherd. Obviously, because he was attacked by a being 11 times his size, the odds were not in Licorice's favor. It was certainly unfortunate that the dog's owner, who was with him at the time, did not have him under better control (another example of when training a dog would have been of value). The shaking and rolling action on a cat's body during a dog attack can cause extensive bruising and damage to internal organs. That's why Mama knew to extend Licorice's medical treatment even though he appeared to be recuperating from the assault. Still, the trauma eventually shut down his kidneys, and the gentle soul left this world. Be advised that, even if a pet survives an initial attack, within days to weeks the subsequent damage it produces in the kidneys, liver, and other internal organs can cause the poor animal's demise. Take an attack on your pet by another critter seriously and seek medical attention and advice from a veterinarian immediately!

Puppy Pal Pointers: Avoid potential drama and trauma; respect the fact that your puppy pal may not interact well with others of a different species.

RW

"The cat is mighty dignified until the dog comes by." - Southern folk saying

"People who hate cats will come back as mice in their next life." - Faith Resnick

If your puppy pal attacks or injures another critter, show compassion toward the assaulted animal and the owner. Acknowledge your responsibility by offering to reimburse the owner for half of the veterinary care bill and making good on this offer. Don't forget about your commitment to pay after the crisis has passed.

Not all dogs are meant to be with kids. Take me, for instance! Events in my puppyhood taught me never to trust these small beings, no matter how nice they were. I'd just as soon nip at them as look at them! Hey, I'm not alone in my feelings. In the United States alone, approximately 4.7 million people, the majority of which are kids, are bitten every year. Oftentimes, they are bitten by the family dog. Ripple, on the other paw, most likely had happy memories of kids etched into his memory during his early months of life. He always wagged his tail profusely as he sniffed their bellies, which were at his nasal level. Who "nose," maybe they just smelled like cookies to him. Given his frail body build and tendency for arthritis as he aged, he eventually was not one for a lively game of roughhousing. The rare snarling lip could appear even on easygoing Ripple's face if he got body slammed by a tot too many times.

One reminder to puppy pals who, like me, don't like kids. They can become very big in a very short time. It took me awhile to get used to Gene, Aunt Joyce's kid. I was pretty tolerant about his presence, but I always gave him the stink eye and circled him like a shark in the water just to keep him a tad nervous. I don't know why I did it; after all, he was crazy about critters and was always rescuing them. Well, as he grew and passed the 6-foot mark, my attitude improved. It's always good to keep an open mind and not judge folks based on their stature just because you were mistreated by somebody of a similar size in the past.

When Uncle Randy and Aunt Melissa adopted Gypsy, they soon discovered that, although she was a kindhearted dog, her high energy level didn't allow her to understand the haphazard motions of youngsters. After a few nip-and-duck (she was nipping and the kids were ducking!) encounters, new housing in a kid-free environment had to be located for Gypsy.

Then they got Abbey, who had a sweet, albeit goofy, disposition. She was just the compatible dog that Uncle Randy and Aunt Melissa needed for their kids, Aaron and Sierra, and their young friends. With Aaron, she completed the classic portrait of a boy with his dog. She could shake, rattle, and roll throughout the house and never miss a beat. In one memorable mental picture, she can be seen flying through the air and grabbing his Boy Scout's cap from his hand as he entered the house after school. From there, the chase was on! She also behaved just like a kid when it came to Christmas packages. There was no doubt in her mind as to which ones were for her, and she would open them with a notable frenzy; again, much to the delight of Aaron and Sierra. Yep, a perfect addition and flawless fit to their family.

Mama's longtime pal, Paula, had dogs and cats throughout her childhood. When she had kids of her own, she continued to have cats as part of her household. Wisely realizing that, in general, puppy pals require more time and effort to raise than kitty cats, Paula waited a period of time before deciding to adopt a lovable, rambunctious pup named Annie, who soon became an integral part of her family. Mama was honored when Paula told her she came to a decision about adopting Annie after reading the following quotation* of Mama's, "My mom and dad had four kids, and they still made sure they took excellent care of the pets. They instilled in me that when you have a pet, it's a responsibility. It'd be terrific if all kids could have role models like that." Even though this was specifically about former family pets, the concept can be universally applied. Plus, a pack of precious pups, including Ripple and I, were mentioned along with this quotation, which made it even more interesting reading!

Puppy Pal Pointer: Remember, not all puppy pals are meant to be with little beings. Avoid unhappy endings by learning about puppy pals' personalities and picking them with your entire family in mind, plus teach kids how to interact with puppy pals.

JW

"Every puppy should have a boy." - Erma Bombeck

"...every man is a boy when he is with a puppy." - Havilah Babcock

(Courtesy of *The Dog Lover's Journal*, Running Press, 1988)

Teach children tips on bite prevention. Let them know that dogs are more likely to bite if you try to handle or play with their puppies when they are very small, run or ride your bike past them, tease them, pull their ears or tail, squeeze them too hard, go near them when they don't know you, or bother them when they are sleeping, eating, or sick. Instruct them not to yell or run from a dog because this could trigger a chase response; small tots with high-pitched screams can seem like prey to a dog. Tell kids to always ask an owner's permission before approaching a dog. Let them know that if dogs growl or walk away, it's time to leave them alone.

If you have children and don't already have a puppy pal, it's a good idea to wait until the kids are older (four to five years of age) before getting one because bites to infants and young children are frequently by the family dog; children under five years of age should be chaperoned when around a dog. If you already have a dog and are introducing a new baby to the household, never leave the baby alone with the dog. Also, shower your dog with extra attention and include the dog in family activities so feelings of neglect or jealousy do not arise.

* Quote taken from *A Technician For All Seasons*, a wonderfully written article by Debbie Ritenour that was published in the April 2002 issue of *Texas Veterinarian* (Texas Veterinary Medical Association)

YellowDog

There was a yellowdog in the field. All the world was a blend of sights and sounds and scents that others could not see. There were birds in the grass and chipmunks in the earth and rabbits near the trees, and their scents wove old, tattered webs across the ground. Each scent was a tantalizing clue to the whereabouts of small fuzzy animals and small feathered animals to chase. And the yellowdog trotted beside me, two sets of legs, a wagging tail, and a lolling tongue.

We had traveled far, this yellowdog and I. We had seen much over the years. It had been the yellowdog that had brought me a deer antler out of the forest. It had been the yellowdog that had eaten a sick mole and gotten sick herself. It had been the yellowdog who had swum out of her collar in a pond. Later a fisherman had returned the collar to us, after it had lain beneath water and mud for a year. The yellowdog had been with me when I had walked past a yard so thick with trees that only dirt grew on the ground. In the midst of the trees an old, worn looking German Shepherd had sat at attention until we passed his island of shadows and gone down a street devoid of a single tree.

And now we were in the field, surrounded by the greens of summer grasses, the blues of summer waters and skies, and the golds and purples and lacy whites of summer wildflowers. And we were there in the beauty of something greater than the both of us, the yellowdog and I. We walked and I watched and she smelled. She smelled scents that I couldn't even begin to detect. She smelled invisible creatures that ran through the grass and made her snuffle around and start up in confusion. She smelled things that gave her sneezing fits. She smelled scent trails that sent her charging forward while I desperately held on to the leash. She smelled, and I watched, and we walked.

Someday, these will be the memories I treasure. Someday, I'll remember a funny little dog that didn't do anything particularly useful or brave or exciting. A dog who simply *was*. A yellowdog who wanted no more than a treat and a kind word and a pat on the head. A yellowdog who gave me more than I could ever give her back. Someday, I'll look back, and I'll remember. I'll remember this day and walking through a summer...

A yellowdog's paradise.

W. Aaron Wilson

(at age 16)

"A dog teaches a boy fidelity, perseverance, and to turn around three times before lying down." - Robert Benchley

"Around the corner there may wait, a new road or a secret gate." - J.R.R. Tolkien

My generosity and tolerance were constantly being tested. It was one thing for me to open my home to Jessie. Then, within weeks of that momentous life-changing event, Auntie Carol proposed adopting a cat. Before long, she had brought two of these finicky felines, Ketra and Cato, into my home. The best approach I could take was to ignore them. Jessie had decided that her role was to be that of "the Enforcer." Whenever those two cats got feisty, Jessie was there to lay down the paw and squash their rabble-rousing. She was like an ambulance chaser; whenever they would get in a fight, she was the first on the scene to intervene. One of Jessie's roles I really couldn't understand was that of groomer. You see, those thin, stray cats that Auntie Carol had adopted plumped up quite nicely into what we termed "little balls of fat," so I guess Jessie figured that it was a big job to keep them presentable, but someone had to do it. She'd straddle over their backs, pin them down, and "nibble, nibble, nibble" with her teeth up and down their backbones. Yuck! And I thought cats were supposed to be the clean ones of our two species!

Just when those two butterballs moved away with Auntie Carol and I thought some structure would resume in my house, Mama decided to start adopting cats! Jessie continued to pursue her cat maintenance career with this crew. Her favorite form of entertainment was playing round up when Mama would call them for supper. As Mama tapped the can of cat food and called their names, their beeline to the back porch would be disrupted by Jessie. She'd head them off and make them run in widening semicircles to get to their palatable destination. What a good chuckle we had after she relented her torment and let them proceed to the almighty food bowls!

The cats did seem to be attracted to Jessie for her leadership. When we would go on a walk down the alley, they would join us one by one. Tater entered the procession from behind the storage shed, Country Kitty from her perch atop the house, Mattie Lou from the neighbor's back yard, and Mr. Black from his sunlit spot of grass. They'd follow us in tandem, or occasionally in two-by-two fashion, as if we were guiding them on some exhilarating adventure. Maybe they just had faith that we would protect them on this exciting neighborhood exploration should they encounter some dogs who weren't as civil as we were!

Puppy Pal Pointer: Puppy pals take their role in household activities seriously.

RW

"There are many families where the whole interest of life is centered upon the dog." - Jerome K. Jerome, *Idle Thoughts from an Idle Fellow*

"Most dogs don't think they are human; they know they are." - Jane Swan

Many people thought that Ripple lived a charmed life. He ran our home, was loved by everyone, and had a family who adored him. He also had the most wonderful way of greeting everyone and every day with a great, big beautiful smile and a tail wag that mimicked the propeller blades of a helicopter. He was, in general, pupular with all puppy pals, kit-kats, or people. Maybe some folks couldn't stand the fact that he was always so happy and in good spirits because it seemed he had a black "X" on his forehead indicating to certain people that they could direct their malcontent on him. Here are some cases in point.

1.) Ripple, Mama, and I are walking along minding our own business; Ripple licks something on the ground and later is being treated for strychnine poisoning.

2.) Mama, Ripple, and I go to visit Uncle Jeff and Aunt Jill where they have been camping at Enchanted Rock; their dog, Klondike, has been running loose there for days. Mama has Ripple off his leash briefly in the early morning hours before anyone else is awake because, with his three legs, he is having trouble navigating on the rocky terrain. What are the odds for what happened next? (In Ripple's case, obviously quite high!) A park ranger stops and yells at them loud enough for campers in adjoining sites to hear that dogs like Ripple were chasing deer off the mountain! Although Ripple was flattered because he never pictured himself being capable of such an awesome achievement being one leg shy, plus he had never demonstrated any interest in chasing deer even when the opportunity had presented itself to him, Mama was in disbelief! The funny thing to me was that, as the ranger was rambling on and on, I spied Klondike starting to emerge from his tent to check on this noisy disturbance in the peaceful nature setting. Before he had two front paws beyond the door flap, Uncle Jeff's hand was seen in a blurred flash pulling him back inside. Poor Ripple had to take the heat for all of us!

3.) Mama always had Ripple and me on leashes when we went to Shipe Park, which was about eight blocks from our house. She also kept us on the side of the park where we would encounter very few people. It used to irritate her that no one else ever had their dogs on a leash, plus they never paid attention when their dogs were bothering other people and their pets. One day a police car stopped, and the policeman signaled Mama to walk toward him. While dogs were running loose on the side of the park right behind him, he started lecturing Mama about the fact that she was using illegal leashes. You read right, illegal leashes! They were the retractable leashes that allowed you, when necessary, to gently reel your puppy pal back to you like a catch on a fishing line. Mama wondered if he was going to have Ripple be part of the long arm of the paw and help him set up a sting on the store that was selling these menace-to-society products. When she complained about this to several people, it was the consensus that it was just easier for him to pick on a 115-pound woman with a three-legged underdog that was on a leash than to reprimand a 215-pound man with a free-roaming Pit Bull on the other more sunny side of the street. We have lots of respect for policepersons and park rangers and the difficult jobs they are tasked to do; they certainly come to your aid in times of need. Ripple just seemed to attract the loose cannons.

Puppy Pal Pointer: Sadly, just as with people, some puppy pals go through life with a black "X" on their foreheads. Remain undaunted when others try to diminish your spirits of kindness, contentment, and trust.

JW

"Sometimes the light's all shining on me. Other times I can barely see. Lately it occurs to me, what a long, strange trip it's been." - Robert Hunter, Jerry Garcia, Phil Lesh, and Bobby Weir, *Truckin'*, Grateful Dead, *American Beauty*, Warner Bros. Record Inc., 1970

"I've been down so long it feels like winnin'. Kick me again, and I'll come up grinnin'." - Steve Goodman

"Forgiveness is the fragrance of the violet which still clings to the heel that crushed it." - George Roemisch

"Forgiveness doesn't come with a debt." - Mary Chapin Carpenter and Don Schlitz, *I Take My Chances*, *Party Doll and Other Favorites*, Columbia, 1999

It must be understood that, although dogs are open-minded toward all breeds and mixes, we do have a certain level of peer approval. Solomon, a neighborhood Sharpei, had been bred to be a medical challenge, as Sharpeis with their saggy skin are prone to dermatitis, plus they frequently can have eye problems (entropions) that require surgical repair. He was engaging and a nice enough pup, but he had an annoying habit that was difficult to ignore. One day Jessie, T.C., and I were taking a walk with Mama and Uncle David. We stopped to chat with Solomon. As we were all facing each other in a circle and enjoying some socializing, a long, thick stream of drool descended from Solomon's loose, overly-skinned jowls. If this wasn't demeaning enough, he shook his head and sent it flying toward all the members of our circle! I know my looks of disgust were matched by those of my other two peers. Contrary to common belief, slovenly behavior is not always acceptable among puppy pals. Even among dogs, a little decorum is required!

Puppy Pal Pointer: Generally speaking, mixed-breed dogs tend to be hardier and have fewer health problems than purebreds; consider adopting one from a local shelter.

RW

"I like a bit of mongrel myself, whether it's a man or a dog; they're best for every day." - George Bernard Shaw

"...a dog can have a friend; he has affections and character; he can enjoy equally the field and the fireside; he dreams; he caresses; he propitiates; he offends and is pardoned; he stands by you in adversity; he is a good fellow." - Leigh Hunt

Certain breeds have been impacted by the American Veterinary Medical Association's position adopted in 1999 stating that ear cropping and tail docking in dogs for cosmetic reasons are not medically indicated nor of benefit to the patient. These procedures cause pain and distress, plus they are accompanied with all the risks associated with surgery. (*Journal of the American Veterinary Medical Association*, vol. 215:461, 1999)

One quiet summer evening, Mama was taking Jessie for a constitutional. As usual, Jessie was on her retractable leash so Mama could reel her in if necessitated by the appearance of kitty cats or kids. They were strolling along the street curb when Jessie suddenly lunged full force at a white cat who appeared from the backside of a parked car! The cat's innate reaction was to hiss with similar full force at the crazed dog in her path. As the cat's mouth opened to make this formidable sound, a small bird flew out of it and made a quick retreat to the treetops! Upon seeing this unexpected sight, Mama no longer regretted that Jessie had startled this particular kitty cat. She told the cat that now maybe he knew how the bird had felt upon such a brutal capture. We often wondered if the little bird went home to explain why he was late for dinner with this incredible tale of survival. We also pondered whether the other birds believed him or not!

Puppy Pal Pointer: In this world of food chains and power pathways, the predator can often become the prey. Treat others as you would have them treat you!

RW

"Dogs love their friends and bite their enemies, quite unlike people, who are incapable of pure love and always have to mix love and hate." - Sigmund Freud

Even well-behaved dogs like Frisky can have
a chewing slip when a pillow is involved

Ketra and Cato may appear purrfectly innocent, but that's not
necessarily so

Pamela J. Wilson

Through patience and positive reinforcement, Grandma and Jessie came to an understanding and developed a special relationship

Frisky George Wilson - master thief

140

Frisky may have been a bandit, but he knew
how to put on the dog in his dapper hat

Ripple plays it safe by staying on shore playing in the sand and
burying treats instead of swimming in the powerful ocean

Decker knows it is safer to lie on top of the lawn chair than beneath it, especially when a person many times your size is in it

Like many puppy pals, Annie fears thunderstorms while Cassidy, the gerbil, is not phased by them

Jessie gains sympathy by bravely reminding folks of her injured leg

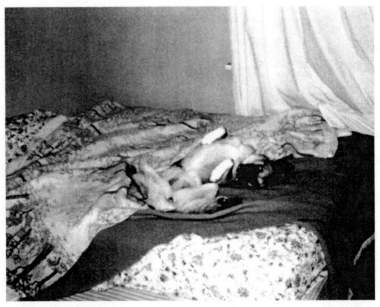

Jessie succumbs to an emergency belly rub, her favorite diversion when she's caught causing a little trouble

Pamela J. Wilson

Jessie goes for the gold as she tries to steal Ripple's homemade bunny from him

Jessie in command of her squadron, pal Pengui and the gang

Jessie and Pink Bunny - some bunny loves you a lot

It didn't take Frannie long to form her own pack of plush pals led by her little pink chick; puppy pals don't require riches in order to be pleased

*Frisky savors the delights of his very own puppy
pal*

*Try to find the dozing Country Kitty amongst Mama's plush pals
of yesteryear*

Mattie tries to pose as a plush pal with her little buddies

Decker safely snoozing in front of the ever attentive duck brigade

Ketra and Cato wistfully dream of lively feathered friends as they watch a bird video on the television

Jessie and Ripple are always on alert when there is activity in the neighborhood; they are very effective at protecting their house

Ripple is compatible with everyone, including Tater and our vast legion of kit-kat club members; this cannot be said of all puppy pals

Although Jessie is aggressive toward cats she doesn't know, she learned to live in harmony with Ketra and our other cats

Pamela J. Wilson

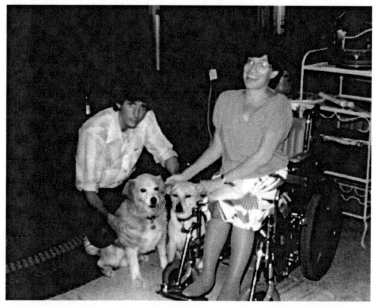

Uncle Steve and Aunt Marilyn's dogs, Buffy and Tasha, are good pals to people but not to cats; exercise caution when introducing a dog to a cat and monitor their initial interactions

Tater may look surprised, but he is ready to come to the aid of others whenever his services are needed

Captain Kitty wisely learns to stay on the opposite side of the fence from dogs that are untrustworthy around cats, such as Frannie, Choco, and Scappy

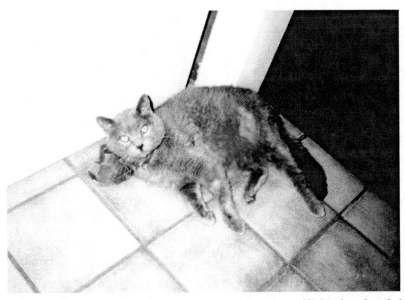

Although sweet Licorice was streetwise, he still had a fateful encounter with an out-of-control dog; avoid tragedies by restraining puppy pals and training them to play well with others

Abbey delights her family with her present-opening skills; consider breeds and personalities in order to choose puppy pals wisely, especially if you have kids

Ketra is a finicky feline who tries to rule the roost; we all need a secure home and safe shelter

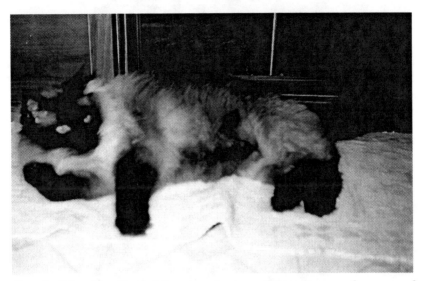

Cato's friendly disposition teaches us that cats can be a good addition to the home

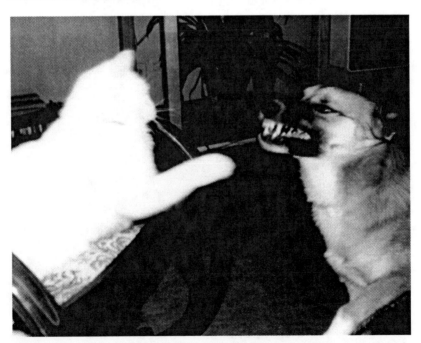

Jessie exerts energy toward keeping Ketra in line; everyone in the household has their own role

Family bonding can occur at the dinner table (from left to right: Mattie, Tater, Country Kitty, Mr. Black, Jessie, and Ripple)

After a busy day of playing together and teasing each other, a dog-tired Jessie is ready for some rest and relaxation with Ketra

Ripple is dogged in his enjoyment of outings, even though he is sometimes the target of malcontents; his forgiving spirit is an example for us all to follow

These folks like animals so much that they dress the part (from left to right: Karen Raccoon, Jan Skunk, Cali Dog, Mama Fox, and Alice Bat)

155

Pamela J. Wilson

Treasuring Your Puppy Pal

Pamela J. Wilson

Ode to Our Furry Companions

"What Dogs Do For Us:
Catch Frisbees.
Keep a night alone from being truly lonely.
Get us outside on beautiful fall days, rainy days, and snowy winter days.
Treat us like celebrities when we come home.
Warm up our beds on cold nights.
Make our hearts more vigorous.
Alert us to the arrival of mail.
Help us live a little longer.
Agree with everything we say.
Warm our knees with their chins.
Provide a use for old tennis balls.
Signal when a thunderstorm is coming.
Help lower our blood pressure.
Test how fast we can run.
Keep the squirrels from overtaking our yards.
Teach us the meaning of unconditional love."

Author Unknown

When Ripple turned a year of age, he moved into Grandma and Grandpa's house for a while. There he met Annie, who took him under her paw, taught him how to run the household, and shared her family with him. I think she took pity on him because he was, like her, a victim of a hit-and-run accident. She was fortunate in that, with proper care and nourishing meals, the limp she suffered from her broken pelvis subsided; maybe she understood that Ripple with his lack of a leg would never be so lucky. I suppose I should be thankful to her, even though we fought the first time we met, because Ripple followed in her pawsteps and passed on her generosity to me. When I arrived in his home, my leg had a stainless steel pin in it. You guessed it; I was another traffic accident statistic who was denounced by her irresponsible owner in light of a veterinary bill. Ripple allowed me into his home and taught me civilized ways and the meaning of compatible living. I never knew I could have such a lifelong companion!

Puppy Pal Pointer: Puppy pals make the most reliable friends to people and other puppy pals; learn how to treat others by observing the actions of your puppy pal.

JW

"The one, absolute, unselfish friend that man can have in this selfish world, the one that never deserts him, the one that never proves ungrateful or treacherous, is his dog." - George Graham Vest

"If man lived up to the reputation of a dog, he would be a saint." - Zanzibarian Proverb

"The average dog is a nicer person than the average person." - Andrew A. Rooney

Ripple was the only one of his siblings to attend college. He located to Southern Illinois University in August of 1978 and graduated in May of 1979. He was always a fast learner.

It didn't take long after his arrival at the university town for Ripple to become the "big dog on campus." Everyone knew him. He would often go to campus with Mama and play in Thompson's Woods while she was studying outside. When she was in class, though, Ripple stayed in their duplex and whiled away the hours waiting for her to return home. Boring!! I'll bet he was wishing he had someone like me with him during those times, but I wasn't even born yet!

One time, Ripple had an adventure all on his own. Mama had to go to campus on a Saturday to study for a lab practical. Of all things, she was learning how to tell different kinds of mice and rats from each other. (For this she was going to school? Any good kitty cat would have been able to teach her that much!) Anyway, Ripple couldn't believe that she was leaving him on the weekend. He looked at her with big brown eyes that begged her to take him along with her. Of course, she couldn't resist. They were soon walking to campus together. When they arrived at the Science Building, Mama put Ripple on a long leash, tied it to a tree, and told him she would be back soon. Ripple must not have believed her because, when she got done studying, she discovered that Ripple was gone! All that was left was his leash. By now, it was also starting to snow heavily. Normally, the thick flakes of snow falling over the grassy knolls of campus would have looked like magic to Mama. This time, though, they bothered her. She was worried that Ripple might get lost in the snowstorm. She ran all over campus calling for him. Just when she was giving up hope of finding him, he came bounding over a hill. He had a big smile on his face and his tail was wagging out of control. He had been having the time of his life! Mama was so happy to see him that she couldn't even scold him. She just hugged him as hard as she could and was eternally grateful for his safe return.

Puppy Pal Pointer: In today's world of busy schedules, make time for your puppy pals just like they make time for you. You never know when you might lose sight of them.

JW

"Therefore to this dog I, tenderly not scornfully, render praise and favour! With my hand upon his head, is my benediction said therefore, and forever." - Elizabeth Barrett Browning

"It's nothing that good dogs don't wear watches. They're on dog time, which seems the best time of all." - Joe Murray

We always maintained complete rule over our home. We had Mama wrapped around our little paws. She arranged the furniture so we would have access to window views, kept her box springs and mattress on the floor so Ripple could easily jump on them to take a snooze, and laid rugs throughout the house wherever she thought we would most enjoy them, such as in front of the gas space heater. Ripple would sometimes lie there until his belly got toasty warm and he started panting from the heat! Everything was positioned in a critter-friendly design.

We wondered why people get puppy pals only to keep them in the back yard. How much time could you spend with them if there was always a wall between you? Was no hair on the floors or furniture really worth missing all those shared special moments? Another point to ponder is, if folks acquire dogs for guard and protection purposes, wouldn't it be most effective to have the pooches inside where they actually could make contact with any potential intruders? Along that thought, why do people criticize dogs for barking when they are only doing the duty to which they were assigned, such as guarding and protecting the house and its owner?

Woof! I guess I'm getting off the topic and on my soap box, so I'll end with one of Mama's favorite quotations. It's from the 1947 movie, *The Ghost and Mrs. Muir,** in which the dashing Captain Gregg explains to Lucy Muir that he was an orphan who had run away from his maiden aunt, and she "probably thanked heaven there was no one around to fill her house with mongrel pups and track mud on her carpet." Lucy's response was, "I was just thinking how lonely she must have felt with her clean carpets."

Puppy Pal Pointer: Let your puppy pals fill your home with their presence; the extra cleaning will be well worth it.

JW

"Poor dog. She's not the problem, you are. You want her to be a watchdog. Watchdogs bark. Now, she's barking, and you complain." - Steve Dale, *Pet World, Peoria Journal Star*

"When she and the cocker stepped back inside, Sidda knelt down and rubbed the dog on her belly. Maybe, she thought, I'm a woman destined to love only dogs." - Rebecca Wells, *Divine Secrets of the Ya-Ya Sisterhood*, HarperPerennial, 1997

* Twentieth Century-Fox Film Corporation

All dogs have unique personalities; therefore, they have different preferences on any variety of events and issues. I loved to have physical contact with folks, especially my mama. When it was bedtime, I would stand on the bed next to her back and sway back and forth until I dropped and slid my backbone along hers. I wanted to make sure there was no space between the two of us. Jessie, on the other paw, preferred to sleep in the spare bedroom, which was technically our room. When Mama was reading or studying, I'd lie next to her and let her massage me the entire time. If Mama tried this approach with Jessie, she noticed that Jessie tolerated her for a few moments, then started to smack her dry lips in a pre-panic mode while getting ready to bolt. Mama used to have to encourage her to stay and reassure her that she would leave so Jessie didn't have to move from her spot.

I loved to be clean, always meticulously groomed myself, and believed in good hygiene. Conversely, Jessie's idea of perfume was to roll on a dead toad that she found in the street. I loved wearing my collar, and I prided myself on wearing stylish bandanas, be they displaying the planets in their orbits, tie-dyed cows, crawfish, or southwestern Indian prints, and always looked forward to having a crisp, clean, freshly laundered one placed around my neck. I looked so dapper in my tropicana-bandana that I was awarded the nickname "Don Ameche." Jessie prided herself in losing her bandanas and looked forward to wearing hers with a splash of mud or a scent of decaying fish on it. She was a true diamond in the "ruff."

In essence, we're all unique. This is particularly important to remember if you ever lose a puppy pal and decide to get another one. Just as with people, there's no way to replace another being, and it's not fair to the new family addition to always be making personality comparisons. That's why it also might help to let some time pass before getting another puppy pal so the tendency to compare the two individuals won't be as strong.

Puppy Pal Pointer: Enjoy the traits that make your puppy pals unique. Love them for themselves and remember that puppy pals are different and special in their own ways.

RW

"Heaven goes by favor. If it went by merit, you would stay out and your dog would go in." - Mark Twain

All of us in Mama's house had special songs, and Mama used to happily sing them to us. Ripple, as everyone knows, was named after the Grateful Dead song, so he had us all beat. However, Mama and our Auntie Carol did write some lyrics for theme songs about Ripple and me. One about Ripple was the *Jeep, Jeep* song (because he reminded them of the cartoon dog on *Popeye, The Sailor Man* who always said, "jeep, jeep"). Another was a tune about his "great, big, beautiful smile."

The doggerel in my honor was much more creative, although I don't think either Auntie Carol or Mama should quit their day jobs to go into the music business. Get this, "Pa-pa-papino, Pa-pa-papino, she likes to chew the kitty cats. Because she likes those, because she likes those, little balls of fat." Now true, I did like to nibble on Ketra and Cato. True, also, that they were little balls of fat. And yes, my name went from Papino, to Papino Bambino, to Beans over the course of time. So, in reality, the words were quite factual. As I matured, I gained the more respectable tune association of Ringo Starr singing "You're 16, you're beautiful, and you're mine" (as in "you're my baby, you're my pet").

Annie's name wasn't in the song Mama sang to her, but it just seemed to belong to her. It was Victor Herbert's *Gypsy Love Song*, and it began with the lines "Slumber on, my little gypsy sweetheart, Dream of the field and the grove." Although Frisky didn't have a theme song per se, he always enjoyed a good howl to *Rejoice Ye Pure in Heart* and ran to join the family whenever *Happy Birthday* was being sung as a cake entered the room.

Poor Tater-Bug. His kitty ditty was simply his name sung repeatedly to the tune of *Lollipop*. Mattie Lou had a much more substantial song dedicated to her; her name was substituted in the title name of the classic Ricky Nelson hit *Hello Mary Lou* (by G. Pitney). Sylvia had her name dubbed into a Disney classic from *The Song of the South*. Instead of singing "Zip-a-dee-doo-dah, zip-a-dee-ay" around our home, we sang the "Syb-a-dee-doo-dah, Syb-a-dee-ay" version! With so many of us around the homestead, Mama always had a song in her heart!

Puppy Pal Pointer: Puppy pals can fill your home with harmony and song, which helps to keep you young at heart.

JW

"Ripple in still water, when there is no pebble tossed nor wind to blow." - Robert Hunter and Jerry Garcia, *Ripple*, Grateful Dead, *American Beauty*, Warner Bros. Record Inc., 1970

Not only did each of us have a special song commemorated to us, we all had quite an assembly of nicknames! You generally name puppy pals when your relationship with them is in a novel, formative stage. The more you get to know your puppy pals, the more names surface that fit their personalities and their various preferences and activities. I guess that is just the nature of the creation of nicknames. Here's a nonsensical section on our many pet names.

Jessie went under the following titles: the Enforcer (due to her regulation of the cats' activities in our household), the Babysitter (due to her dislike of children), Missy, Beans, Beansley, Missy Beans, Tina Louise, Hooligan (we both were called that; I wonder why?!), Moon Shadow (because she leapt and hopped like a fox when she ran through fields, although she has qualms that the song by the same name was made famous by someone with a dubious name like Cat), Peanut Butter Cup (obviously because she liked peanut butter), Jeanette MacDonald (because of her high-pitched howl while she was accompanying police or ambulance sirens), John Jacob Jingleheimerschmidt, Beagle, and Ed Begley, Jr. (don't even ask how that one materialized, as nobody is certain; probably it stemmed from the Beagle version of her many nicknames!).

My nicknames through the years were more reserved and included the following: the Big Ragu, Ripple Dipple Doo, Dipster, Louie, Luigi, the Schnoz, the Iron Paw (because I kept our home in running order), Triple Ripple or Tripod (although Mama never called me that!), Jeepy, Mr. Jeeps, Mister, Bing (because of my howling crooner capabilities), Three Socks (based on the courageous character Two Socks, in the pupular movie *Dances With Wolves,* with an adjustment for my leg count) and Don Ameche (because of my suave sophistication). I was always such a fine blend of famous characters that the puparazzi were frequently pursuing me! Please note that Aunt Anne's grizzly, gruff Keeshond, Shanghai, was dubbed "Wilford Brimley" because of his crusty character; give me my cool "Don Ameche" title any day! Additionally, both Jessie and I went by the name "Angel Puppy" because we both watched over Mama constantly. It's amazing that we ever knew to come when we were called!

When our first kitty, Tater came to us, the names given to him by his prior owner were Garter and then Sader. Given that he was more like a dog than a cat in that he actually responded to his own name, Mama didn't want to change it too much on him. However, Sader was a little too close to Satan; hence, the name "Tater" was born. He was also sometimes called "Tater Tuna" just because he liked to dine on fish! Mama never let anything go unnoticed where all of us were concerned.

Mattie (formerly Maddie), who had also been named by the people who abandoned her at the clinic, was most probably dubbed after the character in *Moonlighting*, a once fashionable television show (the clinic folks were seeing several "Maddies" at that time). Either that or it was because her name frequently reflected the state of her long coat! Mattie Lou became her full title after Mama read *Cold Sassy Tree* in which there was a character named Miss Mattie Lou. It's interesting how books, television, and movies can influence the naming process so strongly.

When Mama and her siblings were still tots, they were asked to submit names in a hat for what they wanted to call the puppy they had just adopted from some neighbors. Mama remembered looking at the colorful fall leaves earlier that day as she walked home with Grandma, who was carrying the new furry member of their family. Her instincts told her to scribble the name "Pretty Leaf." Hey, she may have only been four years of age, but it was the 60s! Come to think of it, Uncle Randy and Auntie Carol may have been older but not much wiser with their respective submissions of the names "Bowser" (this for a dog with the aggression of Ferdinand, the Bull) and "Brownie" (a very original name for a brown dog). As fate would have it, Uncle Jeff's choice of "Frisky" was the one pulled from the hat, and we all know now what a perfect match that was.

We returned the nickname favor only mildly to Mama. Obviously, she wasn't our true mother and we aren't kids in the traditional sense. However, she did provide us with a home, food, protection, medical care, treats, toys, outings, and lots of love. Isn't that what mothers do? So we affectionately dubbed her "Mama" or any other derivative of mother we could devise.

Puppy Pal Pointer: As you get to know your puppy pals better, more names start to fit their personalities and behaviors.

RW

"Some dogs are hard to name and some do not seem to need it - they name themselves." - Ernest Thompson Seton

"I'm glad I'm not the only one who is that crazy." - Pat Hunt (when discussing how many nicknames he had created for his dogs, Draven and Lucy, and discovering that Mama had the same madness when it came to inventing names for us)

"No one appreciates the very genius of your conversation as the dog does." - Christopher Morley

"I'm bein' followed by a moon shadow, moon shadow, moon shadow. Leapin' and hoppin' on a moon shadow, moon shadow, moon shadow." - Cat Stevens, *Moon Shadow*, Freshwater Music Ltd., London, England, 1971

Mama learned early in life to always include presents under the tree for her puppy pals. In her formative years, she even made a stab at gifts designed with her very own hands. She made little Annie a brown and white terry cloth coat. Another year she bought plain Styrofoam wreaths. She then wrapped colorful ribbons of material around them in a spiral while inserting a Milk-Bone* with every turn. One of these went to a very special pup named Maxwell King, who belonged to her chemistry instructor in college. (By the way, this wasn't an attempt to brown-nose on the part of Mama, as she had already completed Dr. King's course; she just always thought highly of people who talked about their puppy pals with a certain amount of reverence in their voice like Dr. King did about Maxwell. Hey, my nose is always black; what does that say about me?!) By the time we came into her life, all she managed to design were our Christmas stockings before she pooped out on this creativity craze.

After that, the appeal of store-bought gifts was greater than the desire to make gifts. Besides, she'd rather spend her free time playing with us than working on projects!

In case you are worried that you can't afford to adequately treat your puppy pal, remember that we are very adaptable and appreciate even small tokens (just make sure they aren't so small that a pal could swallow them). An empty plastic flower pot or bottle can become great toys, and we can have fun making noise by chomping on them. A tennis ball or Frisbee can provide you and your puppy pal with hours of fun and exercise. It's the love, time, and attention that's given with the gift that matters to us.

One Christmas we could not go to Illinois for the holiday. This made Mama and Auntie Carol very sad because they missed being with Grandma and Grandpa. They also missed getting to visit with Uncle Randy's family and the Meeces (these folks were afraid to come to our house because they heard that our kitty cats occasionally went hunting for creatures that went by that same name!). We missed going to our grandparents' house too. It must have been memories of past holidays and the warm feeling generated by them that inspired us to release our differences and unite. On Christmas Eve, with only the light from candles shining around us, we began the cherished tradition of opening presents. After our part in this festive activity was completed, Jessie, Ketra, Cato, and I all got on the couch together in a row. Mama and Auntie Carol watched us in amazement; their hearts were filled with joy by our display of contentment and camaraderie. We had competently completed our mission of rejuvenating their holiday spirit.

Speaking of howliday spirit, Terry and Marc, some critter-loving friends of Mama's, used to design festive Christmas cards featuring Miss Dog E. Face or Tootsie. Their beautiful smiling faces, gorgeous outfits, and gala accessories created a classic, unique look for holiday correspondence. Mama made sure our photos were featured in her holiday cards and letters, too, which always received rave reviews from the lucky recipients.

Puppy Pal Pointer: Puppy pals inherently have the holiday spirit and naturally understand the true meaning of Christmas. Follow their lead!

RW

"Yesterday is history. Tomorrow is a mystery. Today is a gift; that's why we call it 'The Present.'" - Author Unknown (furnished by a friend to all animals, Dr. Alice White)

"Christmas angels flying high light the stars in a winter sky." - Author Unknown (on a fabric doorknob hanging designed by Kim Grona)

* Milk-Bone - a product of Nabisco, East Hanover, NJ   07936

Annie kindly shares her home with an orphaned Ripple; people pals should follow their example of lending a helping paw and adapting in order to live in harmony

Annie takes Ripple under her paw and teaches him about generosity and tolerance

Tater demonstrates the important principle of taking time to smell the roses or, in this case, the petunias

Ketra finds there's always time to reflect while enjoying some fragrant flowers

Like Ripple, Mattie and Tater are easily mesmerized by a glowing fire

Mattie and Tater succumb to the gentle warmth of the space heater

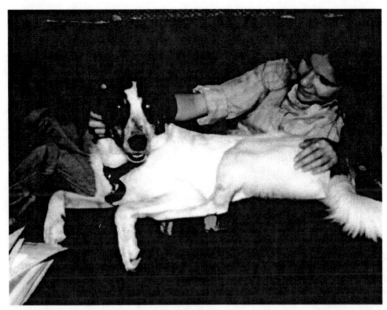

Ripple cherishes snuggling by his mama while Jessie prefers to have her own space; dogs have unique personalities, so accept them for who they are and don't compare them

Jessie and Ripple model their green and red Christmas bandanas in front of the village; holidays are all the more special when shared with a pal

173

Pamela J. Wilson

Jessie and Ripple look stylish in their Howloween bandanas

***In keeping with a Wilson tradition, Abbey wears one of
Jessie's bandanas in Aaron's graduation picture (photo
by Joshua Photography)***

04

Always ready to look her best, Abbey flaunts a colorful bandana while posing with Sierra (photo by Joshua Photography)

Harmonious families have a song in their hearts to relish with others and brighten the home (from left to right: Cousin Bob, Great-Aunt Dorothy, Grandma, and Great-Uncle Clif)

Pamela J. Wilson

For a howling good time, Frisky joins along in song

Hello Mattie Lou, goodbye heart; sweet Mattie Lou I'm so in love with you

176

Tater answers to many versions of his name; as is usually the case, more nicknames surfaced for him through the years

Frannie was named after beautiful Francenia Wilson, RN, who cared for people pals during World War I

Annie sports a new homemade coat designed just for her

The simplest presents, such as a used tennis ball, make Jessie frolic with frenzied fun; you don't have to spend a lot of money to keep your puppy pal entertained

Ripple and Jessie are poised and ready for a road trip to a park; outings with fresh air and exercise are good for the whole family

In true holiday spirit and camaraderie, Ripple, Ketra, Cato, and Jessie put aside differences and gather together on Christmas Eve

Jessie and Ripple are always ready and waiting for the Christmas festivities to begin; spending time together is the greatest gift of all

Annie in her kerchief had just settled down for a long winter's nap

Tater with his stocking waiting for Santa; he'll get treats, not sticks or coal, because there's no such thing as a bad cat or dog

Miss Dog E. Face knows how to dress for a party

Tootsie joyously rings in the New Year

Jessie, pictured in her jester costume, feels that any howliday gives you cause to celebrate

Bonding with Your Puppy Pal

Passage from *Beau*

"And there were nights when I'd feel him
Climb upon our bed
And lie between us,
And I'd pat his head.

And there were nights when I'd feel this *stare*
And I'd wake up and he'd be sitting there
And I'd reach out my hand and stroke his hair.
And sometimes I'd feel him sigh
And I think I know the reason why.

He would wake up at night
And he would have this *fear*
Of the dark, of life, of lots of things,
And he'd be glad to have me near."

Jimmy Stewart
Excerpt from *Jimmy Stewart and His Poems*,
Crown Publishers, Inc., 1989
(a lovely book of poems written by a wonderful person)

Ripple had several jobs. I guess that stemmed from the fact that he was the only one of us to attend college. His first one was as an archaeologist. Once after he was digging in the front yard of his and Mama's duplex at college, he came inside carrying a flat rock. Upon inspection, Mama discovered that it had tiny fern fossils in it. He tried his paw at rock climbing at Shawnee National Forest and excelled in his agility, especially with only having three legs! During this same time period, he became an avid naturalist. When Mama and Ripple's wonderful, adventuresome Aunt Joanne were on a hike and stopped to admire a bush with unusual insects on it, Ripple was able to land on it at just the right angle to make every last one of the tiny winged things scatter. He also briefly enjoyed excavating and would stare in amazement when a trench he had dug in the mud near a creek would fill with water.

Ripple even developed his skills as an expert canoe captain when he visited his Uncle Jeff, who was instructing at Minnesota Outward Bound. After all, Ripple believed in learning from a pro! Additionally, he guided a canoe outing with Uncle Jeff, Aunt Susan, Uncle Gary, and Mama on the Colorado River that ran through Austin. He sat in the middle of the canoe and supervised all the activities, only pausing from his post to bark at ducks or bite at tree stumps sticking above the water. All that was lacking was an official cap for him to wear and complete the air of canoe captain. When they intrepidly passed some cliffs, Uncle Gary encouraged Ripple to bark, listen for his echo, and bark again in response. What howling good fun they had! As someone in a passing canoe said to Ripple, "I want his job!" In his later years, Ripple relaxed and centered on being a philosopher who taught Mama and me how to accept anything that life presents you with a tail wag.

Puppy Pal Pointer: Puppy pals enjoy trying and learning new things, but you need to give them the opportunity to expand. Take your puppy pal with you on fresh adventures and novel trips.

JW

"Your dog is your only philosopher." - Plato

"I myself have known some very profoundly thoughtful dogs."
- James Thurber

Straw had an amazing, yet true, story to share about Scappy. It attests to the fact that positive karma does exist. Straw used to allow CG, an old friend of his from younger days, to periodically set up headquarters at his house. His friend was homeless and was frequently spotted pushing a grocery cart filled with all his worldly belongings through the streets of Austin. When he would take a lacuna at Straw's place, he would sit for hours in the back yard with Scappy and his siblings, Choco and Frannie.

It was at a time separate from one of CG's hiatuses that Scappy disappeared from Straw's back yard. This was unusual behavior for Scappy, so it is suspected that feisty Frannie had led him astray by pointing out a hole in the fence that she probably created. Poor Straw was distraught and heartsick as the days passed and his little buddy did not materialize. Miraculously, another buddy of his, Dennis, appeared at his house one afternoon and guess who was in the car with him? Yes, Scappy! It seems that Dennis had noticed Scappy 15 blocks or so from home. The little guy was walking the streets with CG beside the infamous shopping cart! Just as Straw, Scappy, Choco, and Frannie had taken care of CG, CG was now doing the same for Scappy. Straw's theory was that Scappy got interested in the scents of a nearby creek bed and followed it on a journey that ended near the homeless camp downstream. Needless to say, after the two of them were reunited, Scappy's brief stint of being homeless was permanently concluded.

Puppy Pal Pointer: Puppy pals naturally generate good karma. Be wise, oh grasshopper, and follow their teachings.

RW

"Nobody can fully understand the meaning of love unless he's owned a dog. He can show you more honest affection with a flick of his tail than a man can gather through a lifetime of handshakes."
- Gene Hill, *The Dog Man*

Every night after she got home from work, Mama took us for a walk down the back alley. On one memorable evening, she let us out the back door into the fenced yard and, before she had time to grab our leashes and join us, a commotion burst from the "dog" house. (We never set a paw in this compact compartment, but Mama placed it in the back yard to give the cats some extra shelter.) Jessie had made a beeline for it and was in a fight with a cat! As Mama pulled her away, a black cat, fueled by adrenaline, jetted from the tiny house, hurdled the fence, and was gone. Jessie sustained minor scratches to her nose and ear, but Mama was really worried about the black cat. Anytime a cat is attacked, bitten, or shook by a dog, it can have life-threatening bruising to its internal organs that may not be evident immediately after the incident.

Over the next few days, Mama saw the black cat several times in our yard, but he wouldn't let Mama touch him. She decided that, if he was going to stay at our house, he needed to be vaccinated and neutered. She got a live trap and set some canned cat food in it. The first day, her big catch was our own poor, innocent, wide-eyed Tater-Bug, who happened to be hungry yet again and spied an opportunity for an extra meal! After all, according to the cats, Mama never fed them! Actually, it's a common occurrence when trying to catch a cat or, for that matter, any wild animal in a live trap that you capture any other critter but the one you were pursuing. That is one of the reasons why it is important to check any live traps you set frequently; other reasons include not leaving poor animals where they cannot take shelter and will be exposed to sun, rain, or other elements, will be captive targets for fire ants, or will be without water and food for any length of time.

By the second day, she finally caught the black cat and got him fixed up (literally!) and vaccinated. Her next big achievement was to work with Jessie and slowly give her supervised exposure to the black cat, now formally referred to as Mr. Black. She kept informing Jessie that he was now one of "her" cats. Before long, Jessie accepted Mr. Black, and he grew to like her as well as the rest of us. It turned out that he was more frightened than actually wild. Jessie and Mr. Black would play-fight endlessly. I dare say, he became Jessie's favorite cat. Within no time, he also began to follow Mama everywhere she went, just like a puppy pal. He kept so close to her that she used to call him Mr. Blackfoot because he was always under her feet. Folks say you can't tame a wild cat, but after our experience with Mr. Black, we beg to differ!

Puppy Pal Pointer: Even seemingly wild dogs and cats have the potential to be tamed with time and patience.

RW

"Very few people have the opportunity to know a wild animal as a friend. Except, that is, for our cats." - Marion C. Garretty

"Women and cats will do as they please, and men and dogs should relax and get used to the idea." - Robert Heinlein (Editorial note: the authors do not necessarily agree with the implications of this quotation!)

His Name Was Bear

When he first moved into the neighborhood, I wondered just how many problems would develop with a dog who refused to be confined to the yard or leash. His family had just moved into town from the country. So I made the decision to keep my distance from him. Over the months I noted that he barked at any person, including me, or vehicle in the neighborhood. He soon began to distinguish between people and vehicles that belonged in the neighborhood as opposed to those that didn't. And he was on duty day and night. What a wonderful watchdog! And the barks were different. The bark for neighbors and their cars was one of welcome, and it differed from the bark for strangers and the UPS truck. His dog house in the front driveway had to face the street or he refused to use it.

Two other neighbors began to give him treats when he came to their doors. The Reids gave him cheese and meat, and the Ubells gave him hot dogs. He spent a lot of time in the Reids' front yard as it had the only front yard tree on the block. Often he would sit on their porch with them. It was a special sight to see him and the orange cat who lived with his family relaxing together on a pleasant day. I would speak to him, but I continued not to get involved. Then one day I thought of how he watched over all of us day and night, and I purchased the first of many bags of cheese and beef Snausages* for him. Now I, too, had a visitor who barked at my front door and came to greet me when my car pulled into the drive. I would see his ears perk up as my car turned the corner, and I would clap my hands as he bounded over to me.

As time went by we saw him begin to slow down with arthritis and other problems. I was glad that my front step had been shortened for my arthritis. Now it was helping him. We became concerned when he slept so soundly that he sometimes did not hear the things that he usually did. He came to the door more often and sometimes late at night, which was not his usual pattern. He seemed to be so restless. One evening he came to the door for his treats, and I noticed his tired and questioning eyes as he looked up at me. And several hours later I was told that he had been euthanized. We were all so shocked even though we knew that he was slowing down so much.

The neighborhood seems empty now. We were his friends, and we miss him. His name was Bear.

Mary A. Wilson (aka Grandma)

"Animals are such agreeable friends - they ask no questions, they pass no criticisms." - George Eliot

* Snausages - a product of Heinz Pet Products, Newport, KY 41071

Jessie was always in perpetual motion. She was constantly in charge of corralling the cats and breaking up their incessant fighting. She certainly kept me entertained. On brisk, cool days, she would love to roll on her back and kick her four lively paws in the air; I would sit next to her and bark at her until she desisted. What a nut!

When we went to our favorite place at Decker Lake (yes, the one and the same where Jessie found her very own cat, Decker) or various parks, Jessie reveled in diving for rocks. Mama would throw a collection of rocks of varying size into the water. If Mama wasn't fast enough, Jessie would actually start vocalizing in a cross between a cry and a whine until Mama got with the program and threw more rocks. Jessie would dive like a duck, with only her hind end and fox-like tail showing above the water, until she got her quarry. Sometimes she would surface with a rock bigger than her own head. She would then carry it to shore and have to set it in just the right location. Some speculation has been made as to whether she was trying to build a house, constructing her own Stonehenge, or making a signal for outer space dogs. She built such a monument at our neighborhood Shipe Park that the caretakers began mowing around it, and it became part of the park's landscape! Near the end of each outing, she would carry one selected rock with her until we reached the car. Mama knew that was the one she wanted to keep and add to her collection at home. Jessie also tried her paw at recycling and would pull the occasional beer bottle from the bottom of a creek during one of her rock dives. She became so obsessive about her rock-diving hobby in later years that Mama made sure Jessie had several outings every week to support her habit.

Puppy Pal Pointer: Indulge your puppy pals in their favorite pastimes; you'll enjoy the well-spent time, exercise, and outings as much as they do.

RW

"My idea of good poetry is any dog doing anything." - J. Allen Boone

"A dog, I have always said, is prose; a cat is a poem." - Jean Burden

We all have different levels of citizenship. Ripple was one for answering to the call of duty and always putting his best paw forward. For instance, there was the time he received an official voter registration certificate in the mail. It was completed in its entirety and was quite impressive; the only error we noted was a slight discrepancy in the age they had documented for Ripple. The card created some temporary disharmony in the family because Ripple had been registered as a Democrat and his grandpa was a Republican. (You would think Ripple would be a Re*pup*lican instead of a Demo*cat*!) In true Ripple fashion, they quickly resolved their differences. It was a proud day for Ripple when he went with Mama to the polls. However, before he could place his vote, he was sidetracked by the scent of a sandwich in a poll worker's purse that was on the floor behind the registration table. Now that he was a registered voter, he anxiously awaited being called for jury duty!

As for me, I didn't like to conform. The one and only time mean Auntie Carol playfully tried to discipline me with a rolled up newspaper, I immediately took it from her and tore it up. Another time, when Mama was foolishly considering enrolling me in obedience school, I stole the application from her and ripped it into itsy-bitsy pieces. Woof to them! Some may say that these actions on my part indicated that I needed training all the more. I say that I'm my own dog!

Puppy Pal Pointer: Puppy pals are individuals. Enjoy their unique spirits and don't compare them to each other.

JW

"If you want a friend in Washington, get a dog." - Harry S. Truman

Mama's summers spent working at a veterinary clinic really took a toll on Grandma and Grandpa. Every year she would be on a new mission to find a home for a dog or cat that had been abandoned there. During the first few years she was lucky with her endeavors. Then along came Ripple, who proved to be more of a marketing challenge. In the eyes of prospective owners, his sleek looks, sweet disposition, and animated tail did not outweigh the fact that he only had three legs. After weeks of trying, Mama's obsession with finding him a good home escalated as her time to return to college approached. Finally, worried about her crazed state of mind, Grandma and Grandpa decided to have a look at Ripple.

For his debut performance, Ripple shined. He charmed them both and immediately stuck his long, slender nose into his future grandpa's face. From then on, Ripple was referred to as "the Schnoz." Within a week, Ripple hopped into the front seat of Uncle Jeff's old white Ford, departed from his residence at the clinic, and moved to Grandma and Grandpa's house.

Ripple and Grandpa formed a special relationship. The day Ripple was adopted was July 4th, which became his official birthday. Grandpa's birthday was July 5th. Even after Ripple and Mama uprooted from Illinois and moved many miles to Texas (where they eventually adopted me, the light of their lives!), the two of them would exchange birthday cards and presents. Ripple found eloquent gifts for our grandpa that said it all, including a coffee mug with the statement *Grandpa - with a capital G* printed on it. On his 14th birthday, our grandparents were also invited to a grandiose party in his honor (mine, too, but it was my half-birthday), as he used any excuse to have cake, especially Black Forest. It wasn't particularly my favorite treat, but I tolerated it because Ripple got so excited about birthdays. What a young-at-heart pup he always remained!

Visiting Grandma and Grandpa was always a heavenly treat for us, and we often traveled to Illinois for Christmas. Ripple loved to follow Grandma around the kitchen and assist her by sampling any cooking endeavors, spread out on the living room carpet in a warm patch of sun until he began to pant with heated contentment, and sit by Grandpa in a favorite chair and get a belly rub. Mama took a photo of one of those belly rub sessions and had it mounted in a wood frame that had *Love you...Grandpa* carved in it. It was one of the only pictures that Grandpa displayed in his office at the college where he taught. Another favorite family photo was of the two "Mr. Wilsons" in their gray cardigan sweaters. (Ripple's thin-coated belly needed coverage when we visited snow country.) Grandpa was bending over in his chair with a hand gently placed on Ripple's shoulder; Ripple was leaning against the base of the chair and licking Grandpa's other hand. Life held many simple delights for the two of them! I'm thankful to have been on the edge of these special bonding moments. I think they helped me to realize that I didn't always have to maintain my "most horrible" image and contributed to making me the dog I am today!

Puppy Pal Pointer: Grandparents can be wonderful beings and saints within the puppy pals' kingdom; they should know how to royally spoil their granddogs.

JW

"And Gracie was telling me, forcing me, to stop and smell the flowers. To see and taste and feel the beauty that was there for the asking, all around me, for free." - Dan Dye and Mark Beckloff (co-founders of Three Dog Bakery), *Amazing Gracie*, Workman Publishing, NY, 2000

"Dogs are not our whole lives but they make our lives whole."
- Roger Caras

This section is based on a story, *The Two Mr. Wilsons*, that Mama wrote for *Best Friends Magazine*, September/October 2000, Best Friends Animal Sanctuary, Kanab, Utah (special thanks to Estelle Munro and Michael Mountain for making the publication of that heartwarming story possible).

Alice, Mama's friend, shared a story about one very heroic puppy pal named Sam. Alice's dad, who lived in South Texas, was mowing his yard one hot, sunny afternoon. Suddenly, a horde of killer bees, the kind you think is only in the movies, swarmed toward him. He must have inadvertently upset their dwelling. Before he knew it, his face and arms were engulfed by the belligerent bees. He tried to spray them with a garden hose while he ran for cover in a shed. Sam, realizing something was abuzz, began barking in a high-pitched, monotonous tone. A neighbor could tell by the nature of Sam's bark that something was wrong, so she went outside just in time to see Alice's father enter a nearby shed with a halo of bees around his head. After a call from her, the fire department was soon on their way to the rescue. As they took her dad to the hospital, his concern was for his little dog. They had to inform him that the bees had killed Sam. They say that a dog is a man's best friend. That day, Sam proved this old expression to be true when he saved the life of his people pal while losing his own.

Puppy Pal Pointer: Provide a good life for your puppy pals; you never know when they may save yours.

JW

"The friendship of a dog is without a doubt more intense and more constant than that of a man." - Montaigne

"If it had not been for this brave dog barking and barking to get a neighbor's attention, I would have lost my father as well." - Alice Davis

Frisky Wilson loved to steal. He was a good dog, a kind dog, and, for most counts, an honest dog. However, he loved to "take" small items and refused to release them until a cookie reward was offered. Frisky also loved his grandma (our grandpa's mother), and she had the same love for him. Here's a short story of how these two souls with mutual admiration for each other collided.

In the Wilson household, everyone knew to bury small packages under the sturdier boxes that were found beneath the Christmas tree. This was to deter Frisky from snatching them. One chilly evening a few days before Christmas, Frisky was ecstatic when, along with a gust of cold air as the door blew open, his grandma entered the room! He was so excited to see her, as she had traveled many miles to visit him, that he dove into the presents with a mission. He greeted her by presenting her with a small gift that he had nosed through the pile of gifts to locate just for her. His grandma graciously accepted his gift with an excited, "For me?!" Much to her delight, the label on the precious gift read: "To Grandma, Love From Frisky." How's that for a precocious dog?

I'd like to add my own personal observation to this particular scenario because I was fortunate enough to spend some time with my Great-Grandma Wilson. My last memory of her was when Auntie Carol, Mama, and I drove to her home for a visit. We presented her with one of the finest gifts I could imagine, which consisted of two boxes of Fannie May chocolates. In good puppy form, I didn't balk a bit when my idea of a dream present was handed to her instead of me (besides which, Mama kept reminding me that chocolate at certain doses can be toxic to dogs). I'll have you know that this 91-year-old woman had indeed gathered wisdom through the years. As she sat on the couch and visited with us, she slipped me a few small bites of chocolate throughout the conversation! Yes, I can truly and fully understand why Great-Grandma Wilson and Frisky were soul mates. Who couldn't relate to a person of this superior dog-loving caliber?

Puppy Pal Pointer: Puppy pals are generous souls who understand the concept of giving and sharing, especially with the gift of companionship.

RW

"There's no such thing as a loving relationship between animal and person that isn't special, but hearing Mrs. McGuire talk about Byron I realized that the bond between a pet and an elderly person is unique. Whatever it is, since knowing Mrs. McGuire it's always struck me that older people cherish their pets in a way that makes children's love of pets seem almost pale by comparison." - Dan Dye and Mark Beckloff (co-founders of Three Dog Bakery), *Amazing Gracie*, Workman Publishing, NY, 2000

"In more than two-thirds of domestic elder abuse cases, the perpetrators are family members - frequently the children or grandchildren of the elderly victim - who may neglect or abuse an elder's pet as a form of control or retaliation, out of frustration over their caretaking responsibilities, or as a way to extract financial assets from the victim." - Virginia M. Prevas, manager of the Humane Society of the United States First Strike Campaign (*Animal Sheltering*, March-April, 2003)

I never had the opportunity to meet my Great-Grandma Andersen, but I heard that she was a bit timid around Frisky Wilson. His medium build was a little large for her, I guess. You can image how frozen with fear she was when she met Mander, who wasn't exactly a lightweight. Of course, Mander was drawn to her like a magnet. When he entered a room full of people who were calling to him to come their way, he would walk over and sit right next to her. I personally think he kept directing this extra attention her way just to mess with her.

Many moons before my time during one of Great-Grandma Andersen's visits to Grandma and Grandpa's house, Mama decided to create a little mischief and mayhem and play a prank on her. Mama just happened to have some fake vomit (when you have two older brothers, these items are oftentimes readily available to you!), which is always good for a snicker. Mama lightly wetted it with water to make it look and feel more realistic and then placed it by the cot in the family room where Great-Grandma Andersen was sleeping. Much to Mama's delight, she soon heard the cry, "Mary! The dog threw up down here!" Yep, she had stepped right on it. As soon as Grandma went to scoop it up with a paper towel, the retching caper was revealed. Good thing for Mama that a well-developed sense of humor runs in her family. And, good thing for Mama that dogs are very forgiving, as poor Frisky had been set up as the fall guy in this antic.

It was through Great-Grandma and Grandpa Andersen that Grandma learned about caring for and loving dogs, like their dear Skipper. Similarly, Grandpa learned from Great-Grandma and Grandpa Wilson about appreciating and respecting the human-animal bond and treating all animals humanely and with kindness. In turn, Grandma and Grandpa taught Mama and her siblings these same traits and important lessons. All this teaching of critter compassion did not stop there; it continued to gain momentum exponentially. Grandpa instructed students at Spoon River College for 25 years to respect all forms of life; they in turn shared what they learned with others. Mama followed his cue and taught her pupils at Austin Community College how to care for their and other people's pets.

We puppies send a big "thank you" to our ancestors because our lives certainly benefited from their beliefs, morals, and actions!

Puppy Pal Pointers: Children learn from adults how to humanely treat and properly care for animals. Set a good example and teach them well.

RW

"I care not for a man's religion whose dog and cat are not the better for it." - Abraham Lincoln

Mama always thought it would be nice to own a home in the country for us to enjoy. To us, having many acres to roam in a rural setting would not necessarily have made the best home or lifestyle. Ripple and I tended to be city pups. We wanted to stay inside when our Mama was gone. We reveled in barking at the mailperson, the garbage collectors, and the recycling truck. All three of them would appear on Friday, which made for one of the busiest days of the week for us! We also enjoyed visits from all our friends who, if we lived in the country, might not have followed the urge to just drop by to see us.

Sure, we loved to go to parks and lakes in all sorts of weather. Even so, when we were there, we stuck pretty close to Mama. We also drove her crazy by sticking near all the garbage cans (just in case a snack was to be found!). She would comment on how we had traveled all the way to the lake just to check its garbage situation. Mama would encourage us to run and play, but we were drawn to civilization.

Camping was another adventure we enjoyed. We'd go on exciting outings with some of our favorite aunts and uncles, including Steve, Marilyn, Gary, Susan, David, and Bob. They were all very obliging about having our company on these wilderness trips. However, we stuck close to the campfire at mealtime (who'd want to miss Uncle Jeff's sausage gravy?!) and insisted on tent and sleeping bag privileges. Hey, we admit it, we were city slickers all the way!

Speaking of Uncle Bob, he took the clinic gang to his folks' rather large home a few times for a festive Christmas holiday meal. Willis and Sarah had a white, fluffy, wisp-of-a-dog named Sheba. As Mama was getting a tour of their mansion, she was impressed by the fact that there were little bowls of water sitting on the floor throughout the immense house for Sheba in case she got thirsty. With her short legs, it would have taken her all day just to travel through the house to quench her thirst if only one bowl was available! Besides, plenty of fresh, readily available water is always important to provide to puppy pals. The other thing that made a good impression with Mama was that, in the middle of a formal meal, Sheba jumped into a dining room chair and joined the gang around an exquisitely decorated table! Uncle Bob's folks were definitely Mama's kind of folks!

Puppy Pal Pointer: Don't feel guilty if you can't provide your puppy pal with a country home. There is a lot to be said for city living and the comforts and contacts it holds.

JW

"No man can be condemned for owning a dog. As long as he has a dog, he has a friend; and the poorer he gets, the better friend he has." - Will Rogers

"No matter how little money and how few possessions you own, having a dog makes you rich." - Louis Sabin

"Do not think it is cruel to keep a dog in a town flat. His happiness depends largely upon how much time you can spend with him and upon how often he may accompany you on an errand. Personal friendship means everything to a dog; but remember, it entails no small responsibility, for a dog is not a servant to whom you can easily give notice." - Konrad Lorenz

"No animal should ever jump up on the dining-room furniture unless absolutely certain he can hold his own in a conversation." - Fran Lebowitz

We always thought our Aunt Shannon was one of the greatest women who graced the earth. She was a truly kindhearted, puppy-loving soul. Her dogs, Rose and Sophie, had meticulously trained her much like we had trained our mama. If they had settled down for the night on the bed before she did, she'd sleep at any angle in order to accommodate them. Her lone mission was to not disturb their peaceful slumber. To give her even more credit, we should note that although Sophie was about Ripple's size (nobody had my petite, fox-shaped figure!), Rose was a big girl in the realm of yellow Labrador. This made Aunt Shannon's attempts to oblige the dozing duo even more exceptional in our eyes.

Aunt Shannon and Mama were once wistfully sharing visions of their respective retirements. In both sets of plans for the distant future, the common theme was their puppy pals on the scene. Mama had recently traveled to Sun City, Arizona, to visit Great-Aunt Dorothy, who years previously had moved there with Great-Uncle Warren to spend their golden ages. That city was teeming with elderly folks driving golf carts to a wide variety of destinations. After that trip, Mama imaginatively envisioned living in such a retirement community and cruising the streets in a golf cart with Ripple and me by her side! There's much to be said about the comfort of growing old together with your puppy pals. It's a trusted relationship and an irreplaceable bonding of souls to treasure.

Puppy Pal Pointer: Whatever you plan for the future, be sure to include your puppy pal; you share with your puppy pal an enduring bond to cherish, nourish, and never abandon.

JW

"My little old dog: a heart beat at my feet." - Edith Wharton

"A puppy pal is a lifetime commitment. Although you may go through a period of adjustment getting to know one another, the long-term reward is having a loving, totally non-judgmental, lifelong friend." - Dr. Suzanne Barth

Everyone loves a puppy! Who could resist those sweet faces, floppy ears, and big paws, plus all those cute, energetic antics? Well, I'm here to tell you that I always found puppies very resistible. Who needs that constant whirligig of motion and continual nipping action? When Mama would bring an orphan to our home while trying to find it a permanent hacienda, I'd lie in my favorite chair with my back to the whole puppy scene. Leave it to Ripple to feel obligated to play with the munchkin and take it under his paw. Ripple was ageless. He didn't slow down until he was 10 years old, and then it was only a minimal decrease in energy!

I'm also here to tell you that, as we mature, we puppy pals get even cuter. The white around our muzzles lends us a wise, charming air. (Ripple always had a white muzzle, so he aged very gracefully and never lost his youthful glow!) I went from looking like a fancy-free red fox to resembling a wise gray fox. No matter what my age, gazing at my precious countenance always gave Mama a fine fuzzy-face fix. We develop adorable traits that go with slowing energy and fading senses. Mama always thought my loss of hearing was selective in nature. Huh? What's that you say? Why would she think such a thing? Oh, she thought that because I never heard her call me to go outside on a rainy day, but I could tune into the rattling of a pan in the kitchen or the jingling of my leash by the front door from two rooms away.

Just like puppy pals stand by you no matter what your health, age, or lifestyle, you need to have patience with us as we get older. We aren't being obstinate when we move slowly; we just can't maneuver as quickly as we did in our youth. We aren't being ornery or making a statement when we have an accident in the house; just like people, we can develop incontinence as we age. We need your understanding, tolerance, and compassion all the more in our twilight years.

Our personalities also change just enough to keep folks on their toes. It wasn't until I was 14 that my mama discovered I absolutely loved Chinese food. Yep, I went nuts for pork won tons and sweet-

201

and-sour chicken! Mama made sure I only got moderate amounts of these newly discovered delectable taste treats so I wouldn't end my meal with an upset stomach. I also decided that barking at everyone and everything was no longer my style. I certainly learned as I lived!

Sometimes adding a younger puppy pal to the household can give your older pal company, plus a youthful lift and revitalized energy. It depends on the personalities of both dogs. From my point of view, it's not always advisable to get a new pal just because your current puppy pal is getting older and you feel that having a back-up pup will help you cope with the inevitable passing of the old-timer. You will grieve when you lose your old pal whether you have other animals or not. In the meantime, the new pup on the block will have an entirely different personality with which everybody, including the older pal, will have to adapt. The presence of this youngster can make your older puppy pal feel unwanted and confused by this lifestyle disruption. I'm glad our mama chose to respect our preferences in our geriatric years and just treasure every moment with us.

Puppy Pal Pointer: Treasure all the qualities in your puppy pals as they age and have patience with age-related problems. Also, older puppy pals are very endearing; when you are looking for a new family member, consider adopting an older puppy pal who is in need of a home.

JW

"Stick around any place long enough and chances are you'll be taken for granted. Hang around for 20,000 years wagging your tail and being man's (and woman's) best friend, and you'll be taken for granted big time." - Lynn Van Matre, <i>Chicago Tribune</i>

"Ain't three things in this world that's worth a solitary dime: old dogs and children and watermelon wine." - Tom T. Hall

"Old age means realizing you will never adopt all the dogs and cats you wanted to." - Author Unknown

"Be grateful that your lovable pet-companion has graced your life." - Dr. Alice White

Pamela J. Wilson

Ripple, the naturalist, shares his knowledge of Texas wildflowers with Jessie; a refreshing change of scenery can revive the soul

After his homeless adventure, Scappy decided it was wise to stay in his fenced yard where he was provided with treats

Playful Mr. Black appeared to be wild at first; he was really scared and in need of a caring home

Jessie in rock-diving mode; water sports provide vigorous exercise

205

Jessie pulls and carries large, heavy rocks from the bottoms of lakes and creeks

Jessie meticulously places rocks obtained from her diving expeditions on the shore; perhaps it's another Stonehenge in the making

Jessie triumphantly displays the rock monument she created

The two Mr. Wilsons: Grandpa (with a capital "G") and steadfast Ripple

Pamela J. Wilson

Frisky Wilson is a good dog, a kind dog, and an honest dog, even though he likes to steal

Great-Grandma Wilson's wisdom for relating to puppy pals spans the ages; she and Frisky share a special relationship

Loving parents teach children to treat animals humanely (Great-Grandpa and Great-Grandma Wilson)

Giving families share their joy with all creatures (from left to right: Great-Grandma, Grandma, and Great-Grandpa Andersen)

The art of properly caring for animals is passed from generation to generation (Grandma with Skipper and Great-Grandpa Andersen)

Grandma always treated Skipper with kindness; she made sure her children were gentle with animals

Decade after decade of dogs benefit from parents demonstrating to their children how to be compassionate to animals (Grandma with Frisky)

Ripple and Jessie are earnest in their guard duties and neighborhood watch; in addition to unconditional love, puppy pals provide us with many services

Sophie and Rose are two of a myriad of wonderful beings who have benefited from Aunt Shannon's love for dogs

The grayer Jessie got around the muzzle, the more adorable she became both on the inside and the outside; older animals make cherished pals

Grieving for Your Puppy Pal

Passage from *The House Dog's Grave (Haig, an English Bulldog)*

"So leave awhile the paw-marks on the front door
Where I used to scratch to go out or in,
And you'd soon open; leave on the kitchen floor
The marks of my drinking pan.

I cannot lie by your fire as I used to do
On the warm stone,
Nor at the foot of your bed; no, all the nights through
I lie alone.

But your kind thought has laid me less than six feet
Outside your window where the firelight so often plays,
And where you sit to read - and I fear often grieving for me -
Every night your lamplight lies on my place."

Robinson Jeffers
Excerpt from *Selected Poems*

One year a few weeks after Christmas, Mama noticed Sylvia was losing weight. She took her to the veterinary clinic to have her few remaining teeth cleaned and to have her get a thorough geriatric checkup. Much to Mama's dismay, Aunt Joyce called her with the report that Sylvia had a mass in her abdomen.

After quite a bit of consultation with the clinic folks and some deliberation with family members, Mama decided to forego an ultrasound and opted to have Uncle David perform exploratory surgery. It's barely believable, but Sylvia had a malignant mass that involved at least two-thirds of her intestinal tract; the lumen in one area was almost completely occluded. Usually with an intestinal blockage, food can't flow through the digestive tract; the animal then has vomiting and no stool production. The good thing for Sylvia was that she had just enough space around the mass to maintain basic body functions. The bad thing was that, by continuing to regularly pass stool and not vomit, the existence of the ever-growing tumor was masked. It was so extensive that, for a moment, Mama thought about not letting Sylvia wake up from the surgery. The choice was then made to remove the mass and as much surrounding tissue as possible in an attempt to excise all cancerous tissue; in Sylvia's case, the tumor was too extensive to achieve that goal. Her intestines went from looking like a loop-the-loop roller coaster to being composed of a short, simple curve. There were doubts as to whether Sylvia would recuperate from the surgery or not. Even if she did, the text books inferred that she would probably only survive for a month.

Leave it to Sylvia to stump everyone, including the experts. Guess she was out to prove that cats do have nine lives! She lived month after month, and month after month, Mama catered to her every need. Sylvia adjusted very well to becoming a primarily indoor cat (Mama didn't want her wandering off and disappearing on us if she started to feel bad). Mama also fixed her meals fit for the queen that she was. She needed a bland diet, and Mama was more than happy to oblige. When Sylvia tired of the prescription diet that was recommended for her condition, Mama provided her with cottage cheese, vanilla yogurt (Sylvia loved it, but then so did Ripple!), strained meat baby food, tuna with tuna juice, and a plethora of canned cat food. You name it, Mama tried tempting Sylvia with it.

Sylvia had some wild-and-crazy moments during these days. She was given an abundant supply of fresh catnip from Aunt Diana's garden. The catnip seemed to have an analgesic effect and healing influence on our undaunted cancer patient. She was also receiving prednisone, a type of cortisone. Although chemotherapy had made great advances since Mama had first started working at the clinic, Mama had decided long ago not to have her pets endure any heroic treatment of that degree. A portion of a pill, however, was manageable (except for the fact that Mama was trying to get a cat to swallow it!). After a hit of prednisone, Sylvia would run through the house chasing, chewing, and tossing catnip mice. She reminded Mama of James Mason when he had one of his "high" manic moments while on the then new drug, cortisone, in the classic 1950s movie, *Bigger Than Life*. Usually, though, cortisone doesn't impact animals to the same degree that it does people.

Sadly, Sylvia also needed lots of other pills during this time. Mama tried to crush, dissolve, and hide them in her food because Sylvia herself was a pill to treat. After awhile, Sylvia became too smart for her own good and refused any food that Mama medicated. When will Mama learn that she can't outfox us critters? Mama also had to take Sylvia to the clinic periodically to have her treated with shots and fluids. It took at least four hands to hold this dainty kitty for her treatments!

During this stressful time of taking Sylvia to the clinic for treatments, cleaning up her unfortunate gastrointestinal accidents (which were understandable given the nature of her surgery), and staying up many a long night while subsequently having to attend a full day of work, Mama bonded at yet another level with this kitty cat. Sweet Sylvia assisted Mama with her school studies and kept her company through many a long night. She turned the tables when Mama had the flu and took care of her. She kept Mama's lap warm and gave her comfort by kneading her paws to make biscuits in Mama's thick winter robe. She cured Mama's headaches by wrapping her body around Mama's head and purring so loudly that waves of relaxation would go through Mama's mind. Even though

Sylvia was ill herself, she reciprocated care to Mama. We critters have so much healing comfort to provide.

Finally, it was time for Sylvia to rest. Her cancer had returned in full force and nothing could stop it. Even when the time to help Sylvia peacefully leave the physical world was quickly approaching, Mama would not speak of it in front of her; she didn't want to take the chance of diminishing Sylvia's fighting spirit in any way. It shattered Mama's heart when Sylvia finally passed away. Although previous family members had been buried, Mama felt that cremation was the right thing to do for Sylvia. She commemorated Sylvia's burial site with a white rose bush to represent her snowy white coat. In years to come, Mama often would tell tales of Sylvia's post-surgery months and of how strong and brave she was. She would then end her story by dubbing Sylvia as "One Courageous Cat."

Puppy Pal Pointer: The need to care for your puppy pal or any critter extends not only through fun-filled times of good health, but through times of sickness. Plan to be there at all stages with your special friend, especially at the end of the road you have shared together.

JW

"People who survive loss and come out of it with restored vigor do so because they are able to meet reality with a certain determination and a certain imagination. They create new skills for themselves to meet a new challenge. They grow themselves into new life. This doesn't sound easy, and it isn't, but it is possible. And when it does happen, it's wonderful," - Alla Renee Bozarth, *A Journey Through Grief*, Hazelden Educational Materials, Minnesota, 1990

"Honor your sacred pet's life by emulating her finest traits." - Dr. Alice White

Special thanks is given to James and Sherry Wright for making an extremely thoughtful and meaningful contribution in Sylvia's name to Texas A&M University, College of Veterinary Medicine, College Station, TX.

Appreciation is extended to Dr. Wright for being concerned enough to offer his veterinary care services to Sylvia when the clinic was closed for vacation.

When Mama was a youngster, she became attached to Henrietta, a charming turtle. One day when she returned from Brownie Camp, her folks told her that Henrietta had died. They wanted to be honest with her so she wouldn't always wonder what had happened to the small creature, which was a sound decision. The news naturally upset Mama greatly, but she was able to process and accept it. Even though she knew the truth about Henrietta's passing, for some reason Mama imagined that Henrietta's final resting place was in a bottle filled with formalin at Grandpa's biology course laboratory. Several years later, Mama mentioned this vision to them. They were surprised that she had gotten such a peculiar idea because they had actually given Henrietta a peaceful burial underneath a red rose bush. Death is a difficult topic to address with anybody, especially children. Gentle honesty is generally the best direction to take; be sure to keep communication pathways open to avoid any misunderstandings.

Talk to kids when they lose a pet. Share with them and teach them ways of grieving for a pet; help them to understand their feelings of loss. It might be wise to tell kids the truth when a pet dies; if you lie to them, they may resent you for it later. If you use the term "put to sleep," explain to them that this is different from when they "go to sleep" so they won't be frightened by this confusing concept. Don't try to immediately buy another pet, as that generates a message to them that a living creature has a life of little value, is disposable, and can be easily replaced.

Puppy Pal Pointer: Communicate with children when a pet dies and help them to grieve and process the loss of an irreplaceable being.

RW

"If you love a flower that lives on a star, then it's good, at night, to look up at the stars." - Antoine de Saint-Exupery, *The Little Prince*, Harcourt, Inc., 1943

Go to our "Pet Care for Kids" section for a version of the story about Sylvia's debilitating disease, *One Courageous Cat*, to share with young folks. It discusses terminal illness in a pet and touches on the reality of death in language they can understand.

Sorry for our serious tone and for not being our bright, tail-wagging selves. There's just no lighthearted way to discuss the passing of a pal. The process of losing a puppy pal or any special critter is an extremely difficult one. Certainly a sudden loss, such as being hit by a car, brings its own form of shock and emotional upheaval. You have no time to prepare yourself for the impact of the tragedy. A prolonged death, such as heart disease or cancer, gives you some time to prepare and say your farewells. You can reduce having regrets by truly treasuring every minute left to spend with this cherished being and making time spent with your pal a priority. Put cleaning your house on hold, cancel extraneous plans and trips, postpone personal projects, and relish caliber moments with your pal. Make time to prepare or locate foods that your pal might enjoy eating. Ask your veterinarian for homemade diet recipes that would be tasty and appropriate for your pal. (Mama did not like to cook, but she became a dedicated chef where our health needs were concerned). Nurture, comfort, and have patience with a sick pal who can't move, eat, or respond with the same energy as in healthier days. Even if pals are bedridden, it is important to provide monitored outings to give them a chance to capture a breeze and feel the grass against their paws. Experiencing the freshness of the outdoors can be revitalizing for both of you.

A protracted death brings disadvantages as well. You have to watch your beloved pal go through the illness and witness the deterioration of the body. During a prolonged sickness, your moods will likely fluctuate and mirror the health status of your terminally ill pet. When your pal is having a stable day, you feel positive and productive; when your pal is on a downhill slide, you feel drained and distraught. You also have to make critical decisions on your best friend's behalf, and then hope you selected the right options.

For example, your pet was diagnosed with bone cancer; should you remove the limb? In young animals, the decision may be apparent because they probably will adjust to the amputation and the surgery may extend their life by many years. However, what should you do if the animal is 16 years of age, arthritic, and has clinical signs of geriatric kidneys? They might not survive the stressful surgery, let alone be able to adjust to the loss of a limb. Such a decision was required with our own beautiful Country Kitty. Obviously, Mama knew from experience that animals could get along famously with only three legs. Still, after much contemplation, consultation, and debate, Mama decided to forego the amputation for Country Kitty because of the stressful nature of the surgery for a cat her age. It ended up being the right choice because within a few weeks it was obvious that the cancer had already metastasized to her liver and kidneys. Still, these decisions feel like they are the luck of the draw, and you can never be sure how they will materialize.

You find yourself continually wondering if the time has come to offer your puppy pal one last kindness and opt to euthanize. At one moment you wonder if you are deciding to let go too soon, and that would be unbearable with which to live. At another moment you panic with the thought that you have waited too long and allowed your pal to suffer. Plus, you want to extend your time together to the limit. You become tired beyond comprehension trying to care for your pet while maintaining your job and basic home activities. Being exhausted mentally, physically, and emotionally impacts your decision-making process, causing you to be constantly second-guessing yourself. Try to extend yourself the same compassion and consideration you would to others. Understand that you are doing the best you can under arduous conditions.

Puppy Pal Pointer: The process of losing a pet is physically, mentally, and emotionally exhausting; do not judge yourself or your actions during this stressful time.

RW and JW

"Sometimes I wonder if we don't expect too much from our pets. We push so hard to make them survive because we want them to stay with us." - Bonnie Rogers

"I can recall what I felt when my cat, Jazz, was declining due to failing kidneys. How I functioned each day was dependent on how she was doing." – Dr. Eric Fonken

"Companion animals give us a sense of being needed, of being loved. They are living beings to love and care for, someone to talk to. They provide a source of affection, tactile physical contact, something to touch and caress, to nurture. For some, the bond is as profound as a relationship with a child, or a spouse. Why is it so difficult to understand that losing such an important part of one's life can cause profound grief and bereavement?" - Dr. Betty Carmack, "Losing a Best Friend," SF/SPCA *Our Animals*.

Through the years, we have gathered tips from friends and family on how to help people who are in the process of losing a pet, be it a puppy pal, kitty cat, or other special critter, to illness or old-age complications.

* Make a grocery delivery. Include basics that they absolutely need and would have to leave their pal to obtain, such as food for their other pets, toilet paper, bread, and milk. Provide snacks that are easy to prepare, such as frozen pizza or packages of cheese and crackers. Bring them fresh fruit or vegetable trays. Folks with sick

critters usually don't have large appetites and don't want to spend precious time preparing food.

* Make them an easy-to-warm dish, such as a casserole. Deliver the food in a disposable container so no cleanup or return is necessary.

* Offer to get them some carry out and see if there is a particular comfort food that they might be craving.

* Take them a bag of sandwiches (or ingredients so they can make their own). They're easy to eat and can be stored for a short while.

* Provide them with special treats that they might be able to use to tempt their sick pet to eat, such as samples of beef, chicken, or ham. They won't have time to prepare extra food such as this and may later regret not having the chance to see if it was the one thing their pet might have eaten if it had been available.

* Do a load of laundry for them and take the time to fold it. Washing clothes is a necessity that becomes a low priority when you are caring for an ailing or incapacitated pet. This helpful act will make them feel more caught up with their life.

* Offer to help them with basic housework, such as washing the dishes. A person taking care of a pet while having to work has no time to sleep, let alone do daily chores.

* Ask if they need anything from the grocery store and offer to pick it up for them.

* Order flowers for them to brighten the surroundings for their pet and the house in general.

* Send a get-well card to the ailing pet. This gesture shows that somebody understands and cares.

* Touch base and inquire about their pet's health.

* Understand that they may not be able to meet prior commitments and maintain their regular schedules. Don't pressure them or make them feel guilty if they have to suddenly modify their plans. Their available time is dependent upon the needs of their incapacitated pal.

* Offer to sit with a sick pet so they can run necessary errands, check in at their jobs, or just get out of the house for a few minutes.

* Send them a care package containing their pal's favorite treats. You never know when a pet might have a good day and be able to enjoy them.

* Help them with their pet's treatments, especially if they are trying to do some of them at home or having to administer them frequently.

* Be an understanding employer. Although it is unfair and makes no sense, people with sick pets don't get to use sick leave as they would if they had a sick child. Allow these folks to work at home if at all possible. Remember, pets cannot answer the phone if owners try to check on them from work. Also, owners are the primary caregivers for their pets. It's difficult to find a relative or sitter who can stay with a pet during work hours. Additionally, pets cannot self-medicate; their caregivers must be available to provide them with medications and other supportive treatments. It's also good management, as employees won't be inattentive at work because they are worrying about their pets. Employees will have more respect for their employer and increased morale toward and loyalty to the workplace if they are granted special considerations during this strenuous time. Mama has commented many times on the number of clients who missed spending the last few precious hours with their pet because their employer would not allow them to leave work until closing time. Sounds like the scene featuring Ebenezer Scrooge when Jacob Marley was dying in Charles Dickens' *A Christmas Carol*.

Puppy Pal Pointer: Be charitable and empathetic to those who are in the process of losing a pet; offer them special acts of assistance and support.

RW and JW

"There are years that ask questions and years that answer." - Zora Neale Hurston

"Prolonged caregiving requires much time and energy, which you willingly extend to your pet." - Kathy McCarthy

Ripple and Jessie would like to thank the following friends and family for their contribution of ideas to aid primary caregivers whose pets are terminally ill:

Grandpa and Grandma (aka William D. and Mary A. Wilson), Auntie Carol, Great-Aunt Nan, Shannon, Mary, Susan, Joyce, Anne, Diana, Meredy, Liz, Barb, Renee, Marilyn, Kirbi, Debbie, Pam, Dawn, Dorothy, Dana, Laura, Jean, Snickers, Kim, Sierra, Peggy, Ira, Simone, Katie, Veronica, Rich Ann, Bonnie, Sandy, Patty, Donna, Lisa, Darlene, Martha, Bobbie, Andrea, Jennifer, Becky, Cindy, Natalie, Joanne, Charlotte, Jeanne, Sylvia, Jill, Sue, Jane, Share, Shelly, Sally, Robin, Rhonda, Rosalie, Alana, Julie, Cile, Sarah, Tommy, Archie, Erik, David, Aaron, Straw, Bob, Eric, Steve, Dave, Coop, George, Don, Gary, Dennis, Joe, Brad, Pat, Guy, Larry, Jim, Will, Rodney, John, Skip, Robert, Bill, and Darrell.

A special thanks is given to Keith and Tammy Clark for traveling across town to check on our family during a health crisis.

Appreciation is extended to Drs. Clark, Fearneyhough, Sidwa, Wright, Shook, Taylor, Heather, and Mahlow for being bosses who displayed compassion when somebody's precious pet was critically ill.

Annie

It was the darkest fall I could remember. The days when the sun was hidden behind the dark haze that covered the sky far out numbered the ones when the sun shone. And it rained and rained.

Annie was sick and each day we saw her grow weaker. My whole being was aching with the sadness that I still feel deep down inside. I couldn't even find the energy to bake the cookies I usually did on days when it rained. I just wanted to spend my time with her - looking at her, talking to her, touching her, smelling her. It was as if one of the huge black clouds had floated down and surrounded our house.

Then on a Tuesday in late October it was gloriously warm and sunny and a soft breeze stirred the branches of the trees. Several times during the day we sat on the front porch soaking up the warm sunshine. We sat under the willow tree, and Annie lifted her precious little face to the breeze and wiggled her round black nose to "catch" the scents of autumn. The soft breeze ruffled her white whiskers as I stroked her velvet-soft head and ears. And that evening she ate a little dinner!

The next day the gloom and cold came again, and she began to cough a lot and to grow so much weaker. She wouldn't eat or drink. The expression in her beautiful big black eyes told us that living had become a struggle she could no longer comprehend. So her caring veterinarian gave her a release from the pain.

In the cold misty late afternoon of Thursday we buried her under the willow tree. Dear God, thank you for Tuesday.

Mary A. Wilson (aka Grandma)

"A short time I have to be with you, my love; but a short time is better than no time, you see." - Willie Nelson, *Summer of Roses*, *Yesterday's Wine*, RCA 1971 and BMG Heritage 2003

"Fear no more says the heart, committing its burden to some sea which sighs collectively for all sorrows..." - Virginia Woolf

I remember a story Mama used to tell about a young couple who owned a cat named Bill. They really loved Bill, and their whole world revolved around him. They took him to the clinic where Mama worked whenever he was in need of anything. Sadly, Bill passed away. The next time Mama saw this compassionate couple, their comment to her was, "The only difference to us between losing a cat and losing a child is that when you lose a child, no one asks you if you've gotten another one." You may or may not agree with such comparisons or the intensity of this statement, but you should be aware that there are folks who do.

Mama could never reinforce enough to people that the worst thing you can say to someone who has just lost a beloved pet is "Have you gotten another one yet?" Another forbidden phrase is "Why are you upset? After all, it was just a dog." By doing this, you are callously dismissing the person's feelings. Pets are members of the family and have their own unique personalities. We are not replaceable, nor are the memories that have been created with us. Sometimes we may be the last connection a person had with another loved one, such as having belonged to a parent, spouse, child, or best friend who has already passed away. Again, totally irreplaceable affections and enduring relationships are involved.

We are loyal souls, true friends, and trusted confidants. We pals give unconditional love, a gift which many people are not capable of imparting to others. We also stand by you through lean times, and we don't care about your failures. These traits make losing one of us all the more powerful emotionally.

It's also insensitive to not say anything at all as if nothing significant has happened. If you are uncomfortable and not sure what to say, simply tell people who have had a pet die that you are sorry for their loss.

Many people do not acknowledge that losing a pet pal can be just as devastating to someone as losing a people pal. We puppy pals innately know that this is a true phenomenon. When people have distant relatives they barely knew die, folks rally to their sides and offer sympathy. This is natural and understandable behavior. What's confusing is that those same folks don't acknowledge the magnitude of loss felt by people with the passing of special beings who have been by their sides through all shades of their lives and have filled their hearts and homes.

Some cold-hearted folks feel that pets are expendable and that the person should "get over it" right away and simply move on by procuring another pet. (We've often wondered what the "it" is that people in this type of painful scenario are supposed to "get over." Does this mean you are supposed to simply get over the loss of a special being who has touched your life in wondrous ways?) The lack of compassion that these people exude is very disturbing to someone who is mourning the death of a singular companion.

Puppy Pal Pointer: A pet is a unique, irreplaceable being. If folks you know have just lost a special being, do not ask them if they have gotten another one yet and do not tell them that they should get over it.

RW

"Oh how I wish it wasn't so, I'll always love a dog named Beau."
- Jimmy Stewart, *Jimmy Stewart and His Poems*, Crown Publishers, Inc., 1989

"He spoke with tears of 15 years how his dog and him traveled about. His dog up and died, he up and died; after 20 years he still grieves." - Jerry Jeff Walker, *Mr. Bojangles*, *The Best of Jerry Jeff Walker*, MCA Records, Inc., 1980

"If I have any beliefs about immortality, it is that certain dogs I have known will go to heaven, and very, very few persons." - James Thurber

"The loss of a beloved pet can be even more painful than the death of a person who has been a significant part of your life." - Mary and Herb Montgomery, *A Final Act of Caring*, Montgomery Press, 1995

"A pet that has provided warmth, love and emotional security may evoke a stronger grief reaction upon its death than a relative with whom one has had little emotional support or physical contact."

- Herbert A. Nieburg and Arlene Fischer, *Pet Loss*, HarperPerennial, 1982

"It's strange how the loss of a pet can affect us. To be honest, I've felt worse about losing certain dogs than losing a relative." - Randy Skender

Few moments in life are worse than when you lose a special being. There are some issues that add to the loss of a pet. For instance, often a decision of euthanasia has to be made. True, you sometimes wish you could offer this type of relief to people who are suffering, but it is still an emotionally exhausting decision to make. You must put your pal's needs above your own; you have to prioritize what is best for your pet over your intense desire to keep this special being near you. You want your pet to be able to die with dignity. Trust me; you will know in your heart when the moment is right. Most folks find that their pets let them know when it is time. Their quality of life has gone, and they no longer enjoy the simple pleasures that made their world, like eating and going on outings. Life has become a struggle for the blessed critter. You will also know that this was the last unselfish act of kindness you could offer your pet. Find peace in knowing that you made a decision that, in your heart and soul, you felt was best for your cherished family member at that time.

It may be important for you to be with your pet during the actual euthanasia. Comfort is found in holding the beloved being during the last moments of life. It is a time to recite favorite nicknames, sing special songs, share memories, and say last farewells. Or you may feel that your duress would stress your pet even more, so you turn to a trusted veterinarian and clinic staff to provide your pet with last comforts, such as being stroked with a favorite brush and reminded of your love. Our extended family at the clinic was incredibly sensitive to everyone's needs when asked to enact this role.

After the fact, you can be riddled with "what ifs," "should haves," and "if onlys." I know this because I have heard Mama obsess with statements of this nature whenever she had to face such a loss. You frequently experience guilt and continually wonder if you made all the right decisions on behalf of your pal and if you truly gave your all through the duration of your pet's life, especially during the final moments. You may have found yourself doing something bizarre on your critically ill pet's last day, such as cleaning the house. Instead of accepting that, emotionally, you needed a distraction in order to cope (after all, grieving can begin before death occurs), you feel guilty for spending one moment away from your dear pet during that pertinent time.

It's even worse if you happened to be traveling out of town and were not home when your beloved pal passed away. Hopefully, friends or clinic folks will provide your pal with as much comfort as possible in your absence. You can also call your pet if critical illness strikes while you are gone; ask friends to hold the receiver to your pal's ear while you speak or leave messages on the phone recorder for them to play and re-play to your furry buddy. Still, it's not the same as if you were there, and you can't help thinking that your best friend was wondering where you were during those final hours. This seems to be a stage you must endure while grieving and healing. Try as best as you can to focus on the positive. Relish the memories of all the time you were able to spend together, and keep faith that your pal always felt your love. Remember that the joy of sharing your life with that wonderful being was worth the despair you are now experiencing.

Puppy Pal Pointer: Losing a puppy pal is a traumatic event; try to not make it worse on yourself by reliving the "what ifs," "should haves," and "if onlys" in your mind.

RW

"The options don't allow any living creature to escape mortality. However, we do have the option of making the exit for our animals as comfortable and compassionate as possible." – Dr. James Alexander

"Everybody is born so they can learn how to live a good life - like loving everybody and being nice, right? Well, animals already know how to do that, so they don't have to stay as long." - *Best Friends Magazine*, May/June 1999

"I remember so well how awful I felt when we lost Tina. The great thing about pets is the unconditional love we receive from them." - Candie Graham

"I like to imagine that his immortal soul is now and forever… spirit-to-spirit…loving you, guarding you, nuzzling you, and gently nipping at your ankles." - Dr. Alice White

"What do you do with old regrets? There's a box full underneath the bed, just close enough not to forget." - Donald Wallace Poythress and Leslie Satcher, *You Remain* (Willie Nelson, *The Great Divide*, EMI Blackwood Music, Inc., 2000)

"We are never quite sure how long grief is going to last. We must remember that no two people are the same, nor are any two grief situations identical." – Granger E. Westberg, *Good Grief*, Fortress Press, Philadelphia, 1971 (a book Mama received during a period of grieving as a gift of understanding from Ken Abood)

"You will go through all the many phases of this loss. Eventually you'll get to a comfortable place where the memories are all happy ones, and you will smile because you had such a wonderful animal in your life." – Jean Yates

"Draw upon your deep inner strength to help you survive a significant loss." - Dorothy Simpson

It might help you to read about the stages of grief, including denial and isolation, anger, bargaining, depression, and acceptance. A good source of information on the grieving process is Elisabeth Kubler-Ross' classic, *On Death and Dying* (Macmillan Publishing Co, Inc., NY, 1969). Remember, going through each of these stages takes a varying amount of time per individual; there is no set schedule for grieving.

In the Blink of an Eye

"Beast, Terra, and Anella were my very best friends.
We went everywhere together, except to England.
They had to stay home with some folks who cared
So that while I was away, they wouldn't be scared.

Those dogs cheered me up when I was sad
And they calmed me down when I got mad.
Even on occasions when I felt sick,
Right by my side they would always stick.

They were loyal and protective from the very first
So full of joy and energy, I thought they would burst!
With wagging tails and excitement each morning would start.
With incredible love they filled up my heart.

In the blink of an eye, sixteen years went by.
It's so hard to believe, even when I try.
They were old and frail and not much could be done
Except provide comfort and love in their setting sun.

We had shared so much, but it was time for good-bye.
Their race had been run and the time it did fly!
The loss of my friends has been so much to bear
But our lives together were beyond compare!

I dream of my best friends so often at night.
The dreams are so real and full of delight.
Some night I will stay with them in that place
Laughing and running in that heavenly space."

Debbie Speicher
(critter lover extraordinaire)

"Dogs' lives are too short. Their only fault really." - Agnes Sligh Turnbull

"Such a long, long time to be gone and a short time to be there." - Robert Hunter and Phil Lesh, *Box of Rain,* Grateful Dead, *American Beauty*, Warner Bros. Record Inc., 1970

"If there are no dogs in Heaven, then when I die I want to go where they went." - Will Rogers

To Binkie

"Little Love,
your time is short.
I was just told.
My tears flow
unashamedly.
I love you so
and do not want
to let you go.
And, yet, I know I must.
Twice now
We've tried to stem
the flow
of that malignant
force - in vain.
It has spread
from paw to leg
and leers at me now
from your little head.
But you are happy
and I must be, too.
We will love each other here
as long as that may be.
Then our love will pass over
to eternity."

Great-Aunt Nan Wilson
June 1987
(poet, actor, and lover of all creatures)

"I think of Heaven as a garden where I shall find again those dear ones who have made my world." - Minnie Aumonier

"No heaven will not heaven be - unless my cats are there to welcome me." - Christopher Smart

Great-Aunt Nan has a whole book of poetry, *Growth of the Acorn: The Roots Go Down*, 1985

"Goodbye Miss Shadow, Goodbye good girl
No one can ever measure how much love you've left the world
Every time it rains on us
And we can feel the cool
We'll know you're shaking off from God's great swimming pool
And every time there's a shooting star
You'll be chasing it across the heavens
And we'll know God's playing ball with you just the way we used to
Goodbye Miss Shadow, Goodbye good girl
Thank you for all the love you gave the world."

Pat Green
February 23, 1995
(written for Francine in memory of Shadow)

"She has gone to the most beautiful park of all." - Evelyn Huber

Various caring folks who truly understand the human-animal bond have demonstrated to us how to help people who have just lost a beloved pet. We would like to share some of them with you:

* If the pet has been sick for a while, clean up all remains of treatment in the home, including bottles of pills and plates of specially prepared food.

* If they have decided to bury their pet in their back yard, dig the grave for them. Not only is digging a grave too much of an emotional undertaking for someone to have to endure at that time, they may also not have the physical strength to make one that is deep enough to ensure that it won't be disrupted by digging animals or torrential rains. Make sure it is large enough to include sentimental items they want to bury along with their pet, such as favorite bedding, toys, food, or bowls.

* Stay with them when they lay their beloved pet to rest. The finality of the burial action intensifies the reality of the pet's passing. It can be overwhelming when they realize they will no longer be able to touch the soft coat, smell the sweet scent, or view the loving face of their pet again until they meet in another dimension.

* If there are local ordinances that prohibit people from burying pets in their yards, help them locate a pet cemetery or a crematorium.

* Mark the grave with a special cross, plaque, or memorial tribute. Plants of remembrance to decorate the grave also provide a meaningful touch; roses serve this purpose especially well.

* Order flowers for them; they have a soothing way of providing comfort.

* Write special notes mentioning the pet by name and sharing a memory you have of the pet.

* Send sympathy cards to acknowledge the loss.

* Have a wake so others can have a chance to mourn together and share tales.

* Give them a picture of their pet in a tasteful frame or locket; if you don't happen to have a photo of their pal, give them the frame or locket with the thought of it being a memorial for the pet. Give them a nicely designed scrapbook that they can make into a memory book about their pet.

* Present them with a symbolic piece of jewelry that they can wear in their pet's honor.

* Buy them a soothing, comforting book, such as *Dog Heaven* or *Cat Heaven** or a book that discusses and clarifies the grief process.

* Write or dedicate a poem about the pet; it gives the sense of immortalization for the pet.

* Call, even if it is long distance, to see how the person is surviving.

* Talk about the pet and mention the pet by name. This is a great source of support and a gentle way of remembering a special being.

* Let them reminisce and talk about their pet and how they are handling the loss. Allow them to cry and feel free to share their tears.

* Acknowledge the importance of the pet's existence and demonstrate that you comprehend the importance of the loss.

* Make a contribution to a humane society, pet-interest association, veterinary school, or disease research institute in the pet's name; it serves to commemorate the pet. For example, if the pet died of cancer, contribute to a facility that is searching for a cure for cancer; you can locate one that doesn't support using animals in the research process. It is a comforting thought for someone to know a contribution was made in the pet's honor that will serve to aid other animals, which is a meaningful tribute to the pet's loving spirit.

* Do not surprise them by getting them another pet. They need to make the decision to do this themselves if/when they are ready. It wouldn't be fair to the new pet, either, if the reception in the new home is less than a warm one or if comparisons were made between the two beings. Remember that each animal is unique and has special gifts to bring into a home. Plus, it takes time to build an enduring bond.

Puppy Pal Pointer: Those who have lost a beloved pet may not get support from the outside world; provide them with special acts of kindness and remembrance.

JW

"Ask a man about his dog and you have his heart." - Fern Michaels

"To work with these incredibly driven and powerful athletes was a distinct honor. I have accepted that I must also live with many passings. Tanner, Rasti, Emily, Gullivan, Splash, Skye, Annie, Marco, Mukluk, Spot, Coton...and there are more to come. They give to you, you give to them. There are incredible stories for every one of these sled dogs." - Uncle Jeff

"There are no words for me to say to tell you how sorry I am. I can't imagine the loss you feel or what I can do to help, but I'll be there if you need someone to talk to or listen to or to hug you."
- Francine Fowler

Ripple and Jessie would like to thank the following friends and family for their contribution of ideas to aid and support someone who has just lost a special pet:

William D. and Mary A. Wilson (aka Grandpa and Grandma), Auntie Carol, Great-Aunt Nan, Great-Grandma Wilson, Anne, Joyce, Diana, Liz, Joanne, Mary, Susan, Shannon, Meredy, Renee, Nova, Francine, Marsha, Karma, Ruth, Jean, Alice, Simone, Shari, Jan, Wendy, Lesley, Debbie, Pam, Kirbi, Peggy, Dawn, Sierra, Beverlee, Barb, Melissa, Marilyn, Candie, Janet, Paula, Jody, Judy, Emily, Annette, Kris, Suzanne, Sue, EDee, Angie, Lynn, Annie, Juli, Lou, Sarah, Allyson, Evelyn, Sally, Robin, Kathy, Karen, Jeanne, Michelle, Connie, Sylvia, Oleta, Caryn, Katy, Gay, Carol, Elaine, Verda, Jo, Roxanne, Carolyn, Nancy, Heidi, Ira, June, Mary Jo, Ada, Cassandra, Sheila, Shirley, Cathy, Rich Ann, Betty, Veronica, James, Sherry, Archie, Dorothy, David, Denise, Bettie, Bob, Jane, Rosalie, Steve, Mary Jean, Jake, Milton, Colleen, Rhonda, Matt, Ron, Straw, Ken, Randy, Jeff, Charlie, Pat, Jim, Robbie, Aaron, Robert, Terry, Coy, John, Coop, Dean, Barry, Ches, Mike, Bill, Gary, William, Keith, Gayne, Tom, Eric, Rodney, Greg, Bradley, Joe, Skip, Gus, Erik, Pete, Fred, Chris, Gene, Guy, Charles, Larry, Derek, Jeremy, Dennis, Carl, Page, Howard, and Russell.

* Rylant, Cynthia, *Dog Heaven* and *Cat Heaven*, The Blue Sky Press, NY (1995 and 1997)

Through Sorrow Toward Tomorrow

"When a friend's beloved pet is ill,
There are many duties that you can fill.

Remember all the things that you can do,
To help them see this difficult time through.

Bring them meals that are easy to eat,
Their favorite comfort food would be a special treat.

Be it pizza, sandwiches, a casserole, or snack,
It will save them time that they now lack.

Help them clean house, do laundry, and wash dishes,
Send them flowers or cards with get-well wishes.

Give them time off from their job,
Last moments spent with their pets do not rob.

If their pet must be laid to rest,
You can be there to help them cope the best.

Assist with transport if they choose cremation,
Never underestimate the strength of the human-animal relation.

If the pet is to be buried, help dig the grave,
This is difficult to do alone even if you are brave.

Dedicate memorials or make contributions,
To animal-related associations or institutions.

Write letters, send cards, or make a call,
To help them rise up from this emotional fall.

Let them share stories and speak of the pet by name,
Don't let them be engulfed in the 'what ifs' and 'should haves'
pain.

Don't surprise them with another critter,
They may not be ready and toward you they'll be bitter.

Don't ask them 'Aren't you over it yet?'
Remember this was somebody's cherished pet.

Most of all, provide them comfort during their sorrow,
And reassure them that someday there will be a brighter
tomorrow."

Pamela J. Wilson, RVT, MEd, CHES (aka Mama)

"It is good to have an end to journey towards; but it is the journey
that matters in the end." - Ursula K. LeGuin

"A little word in kindness spoken, a motion or a tear, has often
healed the heart that's broken and made a friend sincere." - William
Wordsworth

I Weep

"I try to understand
The workings of the Universe.
But, I weep.
I don't understand
The 'why.'
I see those
Who don't care about others
Prosper.
Then, I see
A beautiful human being,
Filled with warmth and caring,
Lose her father
And her fourteen-year-old
Canine companion
Within a day of each other.
And I say, 'Why?'
Then I see how
Blessed she has been
In her life
Of love.
So I do know 'why.'
And yet, I weep."

Great-Aunt Nan Wilson
1992
(whose poetry touched our lives)

"I believe your love gave your pup both the hope and strength of resolve to deal with a great many of life's hardships. There is no doubt all the hopes, dreams, and joys that were shared between the two of you will always live within both your spirits." - Bob Oliver

"There is a road, no simple highway, between the dawn and the dark of night. And if you go, no one may follow. That path is for your steps alone." - Robert Hunter and Jerry Garcia, *Ripple*, Grateful Dead, *American Beauty*, Warner Bros. Record Inc., 1970

Be aware that your puppy pal's "siblings" will feel the loss of a life also. The survivors may exhibit changes in behavior or routines. A dog that barked on a regular basis may become silent. One that always slept on the couch may now opt for the bed. They may even prefer different foods than when they had a puppy pal keeping them company or competing for food during all their meals. Be understanding and spend extra time with them to help them adjust to their loss and to a missing member of the household. Find comfort in each other.

There is another direction the impact of loss can take. Here is a case in point. Our beautiful Country Kitty used to love to torment the proverbial scaredy-cat, Mattie Lou. Mama would hear Mattie Lou screaming with fear, run to the back door, and see Country standing a few inches from Mattie Lou. All Country had to do was stare at her; no contact was necessary to elicit such high-pitched, powerful screeches from Miss Mattie Lou. Country Kitty also frequently greeted Mama's car as it pulled into the drive much like a puppy pal would. As she aged, Country became the one cat in the family who frequently enjoyed going inside to curl up for a nap. At least we thought she was the only one who fancied this activity. After precious Country Kitty passed away due to bone cancer when she was sweet 16, Mattie Lou (and Tater too) was suddenly greeting Mama's car as it pulled into the drive and diving in the front door as soon as Mama opened it. She crowned herself the new Queen of the Castle and spent many an evening after that sleeping on the couch or the bed with Mama. In retrospect, Mattie's avoidance of the house was in direct relation to Country Kitty's affinity for it.

Puppy Pal Pointer: When undergoing a mutual loss, comfort and support your remaining family members. You need each other all the more during such distressful times.

JW

"'Just knowing that you're up there,' said the mountain to the sky, 'helps me remember I'll never be alone.'" - David Samuels

"There's no cat like Country Kitty; she was special." - Coy Willis, past president of the Texas Animal Control Association and caring friend to Country Kitty

"Isn't heaven lucky to have your baby's paws walking over the clouds?" – Kirbi Woods

Sometimes during your darkest hours, it takes a puppy pal to give you comfort. Our mama did not cry often, but when she did, it was quite a stress-filled moment for Ripple and me. Mama knew this, so she would try to cry softly into a pillow. You can't fool puppy pals, though; we could sense her anguish. As for me, I tended to leave the room because, being a bit of a lone wolf myself, I thought she would want some space. Ripple knew his place was by Mama's side. If she was on the couch, he would soon be there too. He then would gently place his paw on her arm; it was just the right move to let her know he was there for her and she was not alone. The touch of his large, soft paw provided more pain relief and healing than any medication ever could!

In the solitude of night, grieving is often intensified. During a particularly sad time after our friend, Benny, had died, Mama was exhausted, cold, shivering, and crying on the floor in front of our gas space heater. She happened to be lying on a small fleece rug, which was Ripple's favorite spot in the whole house during the winter months. It didn't take long before she felt the gentle touch of Ripple's paw on her back. She looked up to see his eyes looking imploringly at the space in front of her. She scooted back to provide him room to lie next to her on the small rug. With her arm wrapped around Ripple, she was finally warm, secure, and able to sleep.

Puppy Pal Pointer: In times of grief, puppy pals can be your greatest source of comfort.

JW

"I have found that when you are deeply troubled, there are things you get from the silent devoted companionship of a dog that you get from no other source." - Doris Day

"Cling to the special beings who are in your life and let their beautiful fur dry your tears." – Pamela Baty (Mattie's cherished aunt)

"You will always have your family of dogs to support you." – Aunt Melissa

"If your belief system allows, consider the possibility that your pet has passed into the sacred, holy realm of eternity; thus, having transformed into your everlasting companion, powerful protector, and sacred angel." - Dr. Alice White

This is a tough topic for me. As mentioned previously, we experience the pain of loss also; this can be for the departure of puppy or people pals who have touched our lives. I needed help with the following section from Mama so I could best express how folks like her grieve. She has had more experience than she ever wanted coping with death through her own losses as well as those of clinic clients. She even completed training for grief counseling in order to learn about this complex process that affects all of us at some point in our lives. It sure would take a lot of contemplating to even try to comprehend how much the demise of a special being affects your heart, mind, and soul. I have put paw to pen to provide my best interpretation of her insights.

It helps to remember that, after losing a pet, you will be going through a grieving process; it is a major, life-impacting loss. The pain is so deep within you that you cannot touch it. You see things in stark black and white. The gray zone, where the mundane daily problems of life exist, seems so petty and without importance. You listen to people complain about trivial events in a detached state. Without your pal, your home no longer feels like home to you, which is a very distressing, remote feeling.

You need to give yourself time to heal just as you would if you had a physical ailment. There are no shortcuts to the grieving process. As Aunt Mary G. used to say, "Healing is not a linear process." One day you will feel better, the next day you might feel worse than you did three weeks prior. It will often feel like you are going one step forward and two steps back. Tell yourself to put one foot in front of the other just to walk through one day at a time.

Generally, the first year is the hardest. With every holiday and each new season, you go through a fresh set of memories of what you were doing with your beloved animal at that time a year ago. It seems unbelievable that so many moments could pass without having that special being by your side as an integral part of your daily routine. It's hard to imagine that the same memories that at first make you cry will eventually make you smile. They will even bring you a special warmth. As difficult as it is to lose your special friend, remember that this pain was worth the life you got to share. It is amazing how such a relatively small being could fill every corner of your home and every inch of your heart.

It is particularly hard to lose a pet and not have those around you understand. They have the bizarre notion that your life shouldn't have been impacted by the parting of a being who was the center of your universe, and they cannot relate to your heartache. Woof to all of them! Here again is where employers and co-workers need to extend compassion. Oftentimes, immediately after losing a pet, you are expected to return to work and conduct business as usual with no time to grieve; what a heartless concept! It feels surreal to be returning to a job after such a significant, heartbreaking loss; the demand to keep pace can be overwhelming. It is easy to become bitter in reaction to insensitive remarks and callous attitudes. Try to realize that it is their loss that they have never had an enduring, unconditional love for and from an animal.

You may feel even more lost if, due to the passing of a special being, you start losing faith in your higher power, should you happen to have one. It's a healthy idea to join a pet-loss support group or talk to friends who will truly understand your grief and remind you that you are not alone in your feelings of sorrow and depression. These are folks with whom you can entrust your emotions.

Focusing on work can be therapeutic and a transient diversion from your grief. You will still miss your little love every minute, but it gives you a temporary reprieve from your sadness and direction when you are feeling so lost. For most folks it presents a change of scenery. In your home, you feel and see your pal everywhere, whether eating at the food bowl, gazing out the window, sprawling on the furniture, or playing in the back yard. Your furniture, blankets, and rugs still retain your pal's sweet scent. At work, you don't have these close associations. Take caution that you don't enmesh yourself in work so much that you don't give yourself the opportunity to grieve. As painful as it is, you must suffer through this process in order to begin healing.

Write about your pals. Create memoirs that describe all their features and characteristics. Your eyes may fill with tears the entire time you do this, but it is very therapeutic. You may also want to highlight your words with choice photos. This will create a memento to treasure through the years. You'll be thankful to have it when you use it to revisit roads you traveled together.

Be gentle with yourself. Follow our grandpa's advice; try to do at least one nice, uplifting thing every day just for you. This can mean soaking in a bubble bath, buying a new item of clothing, preparing a favorite meal, or escaping on a scenic road trip. If you have any remaining pals, spend time with them and keep your routine of walks and outings. Take care of yourself. Be sure to eat, sleep, and maintain cleanliness, which helps to freshen your whole outlook and revive your spirit.

Puppy Pal Pointer: It is no easy thing to lose a pet pal. Be gentle with yourself and allow yourself time to grieve and heal.

JW

"Pain makes some people bitter and envious. It makes others sensitive and compassionate. It is the result, not the cause, of pain that makes some experiences of pain meaningful and others empty and destructive." - Harold S. Kushner, *When Bad Things Happen To Good People*, Avon Books, 1981

"Although Sidda was not one to quote the bible, there was a quote from Luke she'd always loved. 'Blessed are ye that weep now: for ye shall laugh.' Sidda thought the quote was lovely and was impressed by its light touch. Luke - or whoever really wrote it - didn't promise you'd prosper or be saved. He promised that if you wept, sooner or later you'd laugh." - Rebecca Wells, *Divine Secrets of the Ya-Ya Sisterhood*, HarperPerennial, 1997

To the very end, darling Sylvia showed graceful courage and enjoyed her toys

After surgery to have a tumor removed, catnip seemed to be therapeutic for Sylvia

At age sweet 16, beautiful Country Kitty was the picture of health until she suddenly succumbed to bone cancer

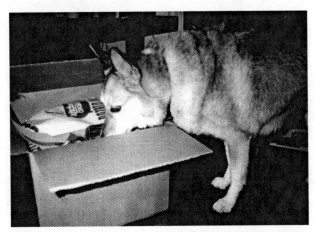

Jessie inspects a care package from Grandma; pick-me-up boxes can help somebody who is dealing with a sick animal

Decker agrees that a care package can go a long way toward raising someone's spirits, especially during a stressful time

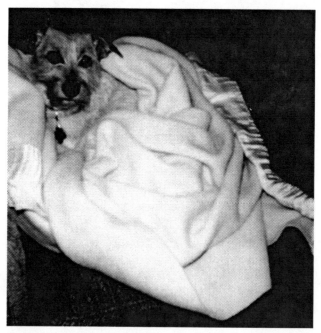

Annie's fuzzy face filled the hearts and home of her family; as you grieve the loss of an exceptional being, treasure special memories

Annie at her favorite spot under the willow tree; she will now always be able to enjoy a soft breeze and the scents it brings

Great-Aunt Nan with her little love, Binkie

Roses are for remembrance; planting a bush in a pet's honor is a considerate memorial

Jessie sniffs flowers from Grandma; sending flowers is a thoughtful gesture to show you understand someone's grief after losing a pet

Anne, Simone, Grandma, Joyce, David, Liz, Robbie, Diana, and Robert realized the deep loss felt when Country Kitty passed away; flowers can express this empathy

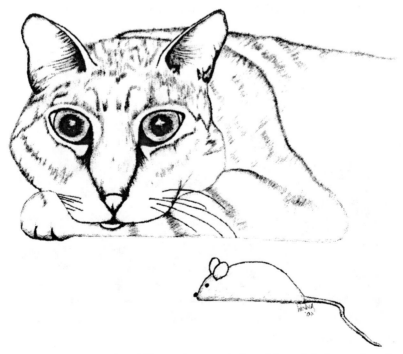

Wendy immortalized Tater by capturing his spirit in a sketch

Commemorations are enduring accolades for cherished loved ones (from left to right by tribute to Grandpa at Wildlife Prairie Park's wolf pen: Uncle Randy, Uncle Jeff, Auntie Carol, Mama, Grandma, Aunt Melissa, and Uncle Charlie)

Grandma by a plaque the family placed in her honor where the buffalo roam at Wildlife Prairie Park (Peoria, Illinois)

Uncle Jeff values each of his sled dogs and feels their passing on an individual basis (Rasti, Gullivan, and Ticker)

Although lovely Country Kitty (front) had a reputation for being domineering toward other cats, she still could enjoy a good catnip bag with Tater and Mattie

Pamela J. Wilson

Critters feel and acknowledge loss in different ways; Mattie had a change in her routine after Country Kitty's passing and became Queen of the Castle

Pet Care For Kids

Kindness to Animals
Think of all creatures great and small

"Little children, never give
Pain to things that feel and live."

William J. Bennett
Excerpt from *The Children's Book of Virtues*,
Simon & Schuster, New York, 1995

A CAT FOR JESSIE

This true tale is dedicated to all the once homeless animals
who joined our family and made our house their home:
Annie, Tater, Country Kitty, Mattie Lou,
Mr. Black, Sylvia, Decker,
Otis, Jonnie Reb, Licorice,
Ketra, Cato,
Scappy, Choco, Frannie, and Captain Kitty

Special thanks to Mama's first family dog, Frisky,
who taught her the joys of belonging to a pet

A CAT FOR JESSIE

Every Saturday morning, Jessie would remind her mama that it was time to go to the park.

♥

They would get in the car, and off they would go. Jessie was her mama's co-pilot. She also liked to look out the windows. She had fun barking at the people and other animals they passed. Her mama made sure Jessie did not stick her head out the window. She did not want anything to blow into Jessie's bright brown eyes or perky pointed ears.

♥

The park they liked to visit was near a big lake. Nobody else went there except a few fishermen. Jessie and her mama enjoyed walking to a special place in the woods. They were always alone there except for the shy deer, swift rabbits, singing cardinals, and mighty hawks.

♥

One Saturday in July, Jessie was diving for rocks in the cool lake. Whoosh! Down she would go! She looked like a duck when it dives for food. Only her thick, red, fox-like tail could be seen above the water. First, she pulled the rocks from the bottom of the lake. Then she ran along the shore until she found just the right spot to set them. Her mama guessed that she must be building her own little castle. Jessie was too busy to see a black cat lying in the sun nearby, but her mama saw him. Jessie did not like cats she did not know. Her mama did not want her to hurt this one, so they went home.

♥

The next Saturday, Jessie and her mama went to the lake like they always did. While Jessie was busy cleaning the lake of rocks, her mama saw the black cat again. He was lying in the sun in the same spot as last week. This was the first cat she had ever seen at the lake. He did not seem to belong there.

♥

The next day, Jessie's mama asked the folks at a bait store near the lake if they owned the black cat. They told her people often would leave their pets at the lake. The pets would then have to try to find their own food. Quite often, they would not be able to find anything to eat. They would also wait in the same spot for their owners to return for them.

♥

This story made Jessie's mama very sad. She could not believe a pet's owner could be so mean. She got a cat carrier and took Jessie back to the lake. She wanted to catch the black cat, but she could not find him. They did find a little bird on the ground. He was a finch that was hurt and could not fly. Jessie's mama put the bird in the cat carrier.

♥

As they were leaving the park, they saw the black cat. He was lying on the cement base of an electrical tower. Jessie's mama took a can of cat food to him. She thought the cat would be scared of her. To her surprise, he was so hungry that he started eating right from the can! He did not even notice that he was being carried to the car. Jessie's mama moved the bird into the car's glove compartment and put the cat in the carrier. She wondered if the black cat was the one who had injured the finch.

♥

Off they drove from the park. The little bird was flapping its wings. The black cat was meowing long and loud. Jessie thought that her car had become a little too crowded! She felt like she was on a bus! As they were leaving the park, her mama saw the sign for "Decker Lake." She decided right then that the black cat's new name would be Decker.

♥

When Jessie and her mama got to town, they went to the animal doctor.[1] There the finch was put in a small cage. They took him home with them so he could rest and get well. The little finch was soon named Atticus.

♥

They left Decker at the doctor's office. He would get shots[2] to keep him from getting sick. They also didn't want him to give harmful germs to Jessie's other four cats: Tater, Country Kitty, Mattie Lou, and Sylvia. Decker would have surgery[3] while he was there, too, so he could not help make more kittens. There were already too many kittens and cats in the world who, like Decker, did not have homes.

♥

The next week, Jessie and her mama took Atticus back to the park. They opened his cage door and watched him fly to the treetops. He now had quite a tale of adventure to share with his family!

♥

When they got home, they played with their new black cat. Once Jessie knew Decker was hers, she had fun teasing him. Decker had even more fun teasing Jessie.

♥

Decker grew big and very strong. In fact, he gained five pounds! His coat became sleek and shiny. All his neighbors soon knew and liked him. Decker was indeed a lucky find for Jessie and her mama.

♥

[1]   An <u>animal doctor</u> is a <u>veterinarian</u>.

[2]   <u>Shots</u> to keep an animal from getting sick are also called <u>vaccinations</u>.

[3]   If animals have <u>surgery</u> so they cannot make offspring (such as kittens), they are <u>neutered</u>.

Pamela J. Wilson

THREE LEGS ARE ENOUGH

This true tale is dedicated to all the animals of courage
whose spirits never wavered when faced with life's challenges:
Frisky, Annie, Tater, Country Kitty,
Mattie Lou, Mr. Black, Sylvia, Decker,
Otis, Jonnie Reb, Licorice, and Rattles

Special thanks to Uncle Jeff and Uncle Randy
for our outdoor adventures

THREE LEGS ARE ENOUGH

Ripple was a long-legged, long-nosed puppy. His narrow body was covered with a soft, white and black coat. There were touches of brown on his face. When Ripple was young, he tried to cross the street without his owners. He did not look both ways, and he was hit by a car. He became very scared and crawled under his family's home. He did not come out for two days. By then he was a very sick puppy.

♥

By the time Ripple was taken to an animal doctor,[1] his right back leg was not doing well. It was in such bad shape that his doctor had to remove it. If he did not remove it, the rest of Ripple's body would get even sicker. Then Ripple could die.

♥

The lucky thing for Ripple was that his doctor tried something new. He did not remove Ripple's whole leg. He just removed it at the knee. This left Ripple with part of his leg, and it was a part he would use well.

♥

During the next few months, the days were long for Ripple. He lived in a cage at his doctor's clinic. He became fast friends with a large, black dog who had been left there for the summer. Ripple learned many things from his new friend, such as how to bark at everyone and everything that moved!

♥

Ripple's doctor showed him to many people. He hoped that one of them would give Ripple a good home. Although Ripple wagged his tail extra hard when he met someone new, nobody wanted him. This did not stop him from always being happy to meet someone else.

♥

One day a slender, brown-haired girl started working at the clinic where Ripple was staying. When she saw Ripple, she felt sorry for him because he only had three legs. When she learned that Ripple's family did not want him anymore, she felt even more sorry for him. She told Ripple that she would find him a home.

♥

The girl soon learned that nobody seemed to want Ripple. She did not know why. How could anyone not love his sweet face, bright smile, or whirling tail? By the time she had to return to college, Ripple was still at the clinic. That meant only one thing; Ripple was now going to college too!

♥

When Ripple was at college, he became the "big dog on campus." Everyone who knew him liked him. In return, Ripple liked everyone he met. He also learned how to do many things. Having only three legs never stopped Ripple from joining the fun or trying something new.

♥

Ripple learned how to canoe. In fact, he became the canoe's captain. He learned to sit very still as it floated on the water. Sometimes, though, he could not help himself. He just had to bark at passing ducks. After all, someone had to protect the canoe riders from such scary critters!

♥

Ripple was always ready to go camping. He had fun hiking through the woods. However, he did not like sleeping on the cold ground. Give him a tent and a sleeping bag any night! His favorite time was when a meal was being fixed on the campfire. He then stayed close to the group so he did not miss any taste treats!

♥

Ripple liked to go to nearby parks. There he became quite good at rock climbing. He used his stump to help push him up steep hillsides or through tight cracks, even one called "Fat Man's Squeeze."

♥

Ripple loved to swim in lakes. On hot days, he enjoyed dog paddling in the cool water. He did not like deep water, but he was always brave and went in far enough to get wet all over. This also gave his legs a good workout. Even though Ripple had fun swimming in the lake, he still did not like taking a bath!

♥

Ripple played chase with other dogs. He would use his stump to help him make sharp turns while running at full speed. He could keep up with the fastest of his four-legged friends. Another good use he found for his stump was to scratch hard-to-reach itches!

♥

Ripple was often excited when someone visited his home. He would become so excited that he learned to jump short distances. That way, he could fly through the air from an easy chair to the living room couch in order to sit in a visitor's lap.

♥

As Ripple grew up, he also learned to like many things. He really enjoyed the holidays. Ones with treats were his favorites, such as Easter, Halloween, and Christmas. Birthdays were special because of the cake and ice cream. He even had his own party every year. His sister, Jessie, his best friend, a Pekinese named T.C., and his Uncle David were always invited.

♥

It was not long before the girl who belonged to Ripple no longer felt sorry for him. For one thing, Ripple never felt sorry for himself. For another, she knew that he was living a full life. She loved Ripple for just being Ripple.

273

♥

Sometimes people who saw Ripple for the first time would say, "Oh, what a poor dog." Then the girl would tell them about how happy Ripple was. After they were around him, they soon would see that having only three legs did not matter to Ripple. He was always ready to have fun and spend time with his many friends.

♥

For the rest of her life, the girl was thankful that she had shared her heart and home with Ripple. After all, he was the best thing that had ever happened to her!

♥

[1] An <u>animal doctor</u> is a <u>veterinarian</u>

ONE COURAGEOUS CAT

Pamela J. Wilson

This true tale is dedicated to the strong-willed animals
who maintained a courageous, yet gentle, spirit:
Frisky, Annie, Tater, Country Kitty,
Mattie Lou, Mr. Black, Sylvia, Decker,
Otis, Jonnie Reb, Licorice,
Mattie-Look-Alike-Kitty,
Ketra, Cato, Binkie, Cleo, and Abbey

Special thanks to Joyce, David, Anne, Liz, Coop, and Gene
who helped Sylvia to not only survive, but thrive

ONE COURAGEOUS CAT

The brown-haired girl opened her door. She was still in the blue dress she had worn to work that day. There, standing in front of her, was her neighbor. He was holding a cat that was white with patches of gray stripes. He did not know this cat. He did not even know where she lived. She had just landed on his doorstep. She was hurt, and he did not want her. He was hoping that the girl would take care of her.

♥

The cat was quite a mess. She was old, and her face had a nasty sore on it. The sore was caused from a bad tooth. The girl took her to an animal doctor's[1] office so she could be cleaned up. Her sore and her bad tooth were also treated. The cat seemed happy to have someone take care of her.

♥

Next, the girl looked for the cat's owners, but she could not find them. After many days, she knew that she needed to find the cat a new home. The cat was not a pretty kitty at that time, so the girl felt that nobody would want her. She decided to keep the cat. She named her Sylvia.

♥

Sylvia soon felt at home at the girl's house. She soon also felt good enough to start fights with the girl's other cats, Tater, Country Kitty, and Mattie Lou. Sylvia's sore even got better. Underneath it was a sweet face with lovely gray-striped markings. In fact, Sylvia went from being quite a mess to being quite a beauty.

♥

Sylvia was given many nicknames by the girl and the girl's mother who liked to visit her grandkitties. They would call her names like Syb-a-dee, Sybbie, Syb, and Tibbs. They would also sing "Syb-a-dee-doo-dah, Syb-a-dee-ay" to her all the time. She was indeed part of the girl's family now.

♥

Sylvia loved to get on the roof, but she could not always get off of it. Nobody was quite sure why she could move upward but not downward. The girl or the girl's friends had to climb on the roof to get her. Silly Sybbie would roll over on her back until they got near her. Then she would run and try to hide from them under the

rain gutter.

♥

One Christmas, Sylvia would not let anyone catch her on the

roof. The girl had to set her Christmas treats and presents, such as a

catnip mouse, on the roof. She hoped Sylvia would be able to enjoy

them anyway. After all, she had been a good girl all year long!

♥

Shortly after that Christmas, the girl thought Sylvia looked

thin. She took her to the animal doctor's office for a checkup. The

girl soon learned that Sylvia was losing weight because she had a

growth. It was in the area where food went to be made usable by

her body.[2]

♥

Sylvia had surgery to have the growth removed. Tests were then

done on her growth. The tests showed that the growth would not

go away and that it would return. The girl was told that Sylvia had

cancer.[3] The girl was also told that Sylvia may only live for one

month. This news made the girl cry and feel very sad.

♥

The girl took Sylvia home to get better after her surgery. Sylvia got much medicine at first. She had to have water put in her body through a needle. She also had lots of shots in her back legs and pills poked down her throat. Sylvia did not take this lightly. She became quite feisty and fought with everyone who tried to treat her! Small as she was, four hands were needed just to give her a pill!

♥

The girl would crush Sylvia's pills into tiny pieces. Then she would mix them in meaty gravy. At first, Sylvia liked her pills fixed this way. After awhile, though, she seemed to know when pills were put in her food. Then she would walk away and leave her dish full of food. Sometimes Sylvia was too smart for her own good!

♥

When Sylvia was not being treated, she was very, very sweet. She got better after her surgery and did not have to get so many shots or pills. This made Sylvia very happy. If Sylvia was happy, the girl was happy.

♥

Sylvia had to have certain foods because of her surgery. She really did not mind this so much. The girl tried to make everything taste good to her. In addition to special cat food from the animal doctor's office, Sylvia enjoyed eating cottage cheese and vanilla yogurt. It was not long before she gained back the weight she had lost.

♥

Even though she liked her new food, Sylvia would sometimes nibble on the bag of dry food that was for the other cats. She would chew a hole in it just like a little mouse. The girl would not get mad at her for munching a bite or two of this food. She felt Sylvia should have whatever she wanted.

♥

The girl now kept Sylvia inside most of the time because she did not want her to get on the roof. This, too, Sylvia did not seem to mind. She had fun being a house cat. She moved in and took over the house. Everything down to the last knickknack was placed to make Sylvia cozy.

♥

When the girl was sick, Sylvia, in turn, took care of her. She would lie on the girl's lap all day to keep her company. Sylvia and the girl even took catnaps together. Sylvia also curled her toes and kneaded her paws to "make biscuits" in the girl's thick winter robe. This made them both content and restful.

♥

Sylvia and the girl were very close to each other. Sylvia joined the girl during her workouts each day. She studied with her every night. Sylvia even slept with the girl. She would often gently place one of her front paws on the girl's cheek or arm. She would wrap her body around the girl's head and purr. Her purring was so loud that waves from it gently rolled through the girl's head. It helped both of them to relax.

♥

In the southern state where Sylvia lived, there were really big pests called cockroaches. If one of these pesky pests tried to sneak into Sylvia's home at night, she showed no fear. Surgery or no surgery, she would stalk it. Sylvia proudly guarded the girl's bedroom against such nasty critters. She was indeed the "Mighty Huntress."

♥

Sylvia had many duties. Every morning at 5:30 she gave the girl a wake-up call. She dug her nails into the bed sheets and quickly pulled them out again. The girl woke to the sound of "kerrr, kerrr, kerrr" as the sheets pulled from Sylvia's nails. When the girl saw Sylvia's sweet face, she would smile and say, "Good morning, Angelface!"

♥

Sylvia even helped the girl get ready for work in the morning. She would sit on the toilet by the tub while the girl took a shower. When the shower curtain opened, Sylvia would jump into the tub. She liked to lick the water from its cool surface. The girl would leave cold water dripping just for Sylvia. Other than that, Sylvia most certainly did not like baths!

♥

Sylvia was not always quiet. She loved to play with catnip toys and eat fresh catnip. Sometimes, after enjoying one of these treats, she would race through the house like a crazy cat. She would act so wild that she made the girl laugh. She was glad that Sylvia felt good again. Her favorite thing to say to her was, "Sybbie, you are so dang cute!"

♥

Sadly, Sylvia did not always feel like racing and playing or even eating. At these times, she had to be treated by the animal doctor and the girl. Again, four hands were needed! It was hard to decide to give her more shots and pills, but the girl knew that it was best for Sylvia. Even when Sylvia was not feeling well, she purred sweetly and "made biscuits" with her paws when she was at home.

♥

Sylvia lived for many, many months after her surgery before she passed away. She was always brave and stayed full of spirit. The girl loved every minute that she had gotten to spend with her. In memory of Sylvia, the girl planted a white rose bush over her grave. Whenever the girl thought of all Sylvia had gone through, she would say, "You were one courageous cat!"

♥

¹   An <u>animal doctor</u> is a <u>veterinarian</u>.

²   The <u>area</u> meant here where food goes to be made usable by the body is the <u>intestinal tract</u>.

³   <u>Cancer</u> is a type of new <u>growth</u> that animals can get in their bodies. It can sometimes make animals very sick. Animals can even die when they have certain types of cancer.

Otis and the Mockingbirds

Pamela J. Wilson

This story is dedicated to
all creatures great and small

Special thanks to
Tater, Country Kitty, Mattie Lou, Mr. Black,
Sylvia, Decker, Ellen, Jonnie Reb,
Licorice, Poof Muffin, and Cupcake,
who helped pave the way for a place Otis could call home

Otis and the Mockingbirds

Tater, Mattie, and Decker used to eat their breakfast on the back porch step. One day, a very thin, lanky brown tabby joined them for a meal. These three cats were not pleased when their mama gave this strange cat some of their food to eat.

♥

The next day, the same cat stopped by for another meal. He did it again the day after that. The brown tabby was so thin that their mama felt sorry for him. She even called him "Skinny Man." Still, Tater, Mattie, and Decker were not happy about sharing their food with him.

♥

When "Skinny Man" kept stopping by for meals, their mama decided that he was a keeper. She went to the animal clinic to see about getting him vaccinated[1] and neutered[2] so he could not help to make any kittens. After all, there were already too many cats in the world who did not have homes. The clinic was across the alley that was behind the house where the three cats lived.

♥

Their mama soon learned that the folks at the clinic also knew this brown tabby. They had been calling him "Skinny Mon." They had just vaccinated and neutered him. He had been getting food from them too.

♥

This clever cat was spending his nights romping outside. That was why he was always at breakfast with the other three cats. After he ate, he ran across the alley and pawed at the door of the animal clinic. When they let him inside, he would hop in a cage and sleep the day away. He also enjoyed more food while he was there. With so many meals in his growing tummy, the names "Skinny Man" and "Skinny Mon" no longer fit him. Everyone finally agreed that a good name for him was Otis.

♥

One fine day two mockingbirds[3] got very mad at Otis. Chances are that he caused some trouble for them! Cats, by nature, hunt birds. Maybe he had hurt one of their babies. These two birds waited and watched for Otis. When they spied him, they would attack. The hunter was now the hunted.

♥

The mockingbirds would perch on high places and wait for him to place a paw outside the clinic door. Oftentimes, two tiny heads were seen peering at Otis from the clinic's roof ledge. As soon as he tried to cross the alley, they would strike.

♥

First, the mockingbirds would dive at him. When they felt brave, they would peck his hind end with their beaks. If he kept walking, they would ride on his back. Their wings would be wildly flapping up and down the whole time.

♥

Otis took all this in stride. Maybe he knew he had done something to deserve it! Although he was neutered, Otis often fought with other cats, especially Decker. For some reason, though, he let the mockingbirds pester him. He never even swatted at them.

♥

The mockingbirds squawked very loudly whenever they saw Otis. Their screeches were so loud that everyone in the neighborhood knew when Otis was coming. Even Decker learned that the mockingbird's trill meant that Otis was nearby. Decker then knew to get ready to either run or fight with this bully.

♥

This action kept up all summer long. Finally, Otis got some peace. All winter it was quiet. Then, as spring sprung, a noisy sound was heard and silly sight was seen. There was squawking at Tater, Mattie, and Decker's front door. When the door was opened, there stood Otis. He was not alone. There was also a mockingbird hovering under the porch archway. With every chance she got, the bird swooped down and pecked the hind end of Otis. As with last year, Otis would spend his summer vacation with his feisty feathered friends.

♥

[1]   Vaccinations are shots to keep an animal from getting sick.

[2]   If animals are neutered, they had surgery so they cannot make offspring (such as kittens).

[3]   A mockingbird is the state bird of Texas, which is where Otis lived.

"Tra-la-la, Twiddle-dee-dee-dee, It gives me a thrill, To wake up in the morning to the mockingbird's trill. Tra-la-la, Twiddle-dee-dee-dee, There's peace and goodwill. You're welcome as the flowers on Mockingbird Hill." - chorus to an old tune sung as an "Ode to Otis" by Grandma

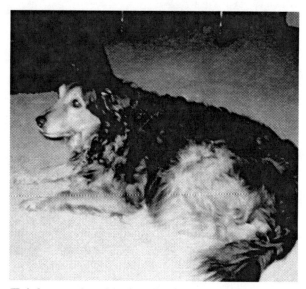

Frisky teaches his family the joys of belonging to a pet

A dog completes the picture of a happy household (the Wilson kids from left to right: back – Auntie Carol and Uncle Randy; front – Mama, Frisky, and Uncle Jeff)

With his calm ways, Tater inspires Mama to adopt more cats

Jonnie Reb, a once homeless cat who had been living paw-to-mouth, touches our home with her gentle ways

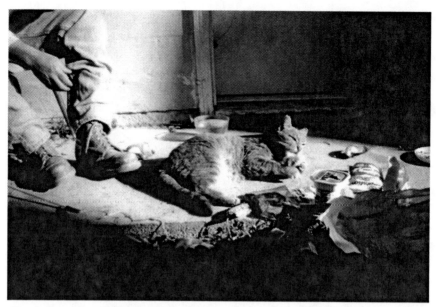

Cool Captain Kitty quickly learns that a home where he receives Christmas presents is much better than living on the street doing the stray cat strut

Whoosh! Jessie dives like a duck for rocks with only her tail above the water; it feels so good to be active

Jessie always finds rocks during her dives and brings them to shore; she stays busy during her outings

Decker Lake is a perfect place for Jessie to enjoy the wildflowers; new scents and changes in scenery are good for the spirit

After rescuing him from being homeless at the lake, Decker became one of Jessie's favorite cats; Jessie and Uncle David share treats with this slender orphan

With lots of love and good food in his new home, Decker was soon sassy and full-bellied; animals trust you with their care, so it's never right to desert them

*By Decker's first Christmas, he was feisty, healthy, and happy
(pictured here with Sylvia); everybody needs a safe place to call
home*

*Decker joins the rest of the kit-kat club in their present-opening
activities (from left to right: Mama, Country Kitty, Mattie,
Decker, and Tater)*

Grandma and Decker (seen here with rabbit ears) share many playful moments

Ripple likes to go to parks for fresh air and exercise, which help to keep him healthy

Swimming feels good to Ripple; it also helps him to relax and keep cool

When Jessie and Ripple put on their party hats, they are ready for friends, fun, and food; a dog's life should not be ruff!

Jessie and T.C. dress up in ribbons and bows for parties; happy times are even more fun when shared with others

Jessie helps Ripple open his presents; Ripple watches this activity to make sure everybody gets a treat

Ripple is a thankful addition to his family; adopting a dog brings much joy

Sylvia napping on her Grandma's lap (Country Kitty to the side in her favorite basket)

Pamela J. Wilson

For a sick animal like Sylvia, it helps to try different foods that are tempting, tasty, and easy to eat

Even when she is ill, Sylvia takes time to help with study sessions; your pets are always by your side, so do the same for them during times of good health and of sickness

After working hard at being a bookmark, silly Sylvia earns some rest

Poof Muffin is one of many neighboring cats who enjoy free chow at our house; be kind to all creatures great and small

Although they aren't happy about it, the other cats let Otis join them for a meal (from left to right: Tater, Otis, Mattie, and Decker)

Between the clinic and our house, Otis never went hungry; he also received proper care by getting his shots and being neutered so he couldn't help make more homeless cats

The mockingbird does not trust or like Otis; this angry bird flaps above him, screeches at him, and follows him everywhere

The mad mockingbird rides on the tail end of Otis and pecks at him; even though cats hunt birds, Otis never fights back

Meeting the Puppy Pal Players

Pamela J. Wilson

Cast of Canine Characters and Crew

Puppy Pal Pack

Abbey (aka YellowDog, Woof):
artistic attributes - yellow Labrador Retriever
lineage links - our non-blood canine cousin; belongs with Uncle Randy, Aunt Melissa, and their kids, Aaron and Sierra
fascinating facts - name associated with the Beatles' *Abbey Road*; sweet-natured with a zest for life when opening presents and sneaking snacks; reportedly absconded with a whole cheesecake; exuberant; friendly disposition to all

Annie (aka Bodine, Annie Baby, Shortcakes, Beauts, Shavetail, Miss Demando):
artistic attributes – cute terrier cross; light brown, bristly coat with velvet-soft ears
lineage links - belongs with Grandma and Grandpa
fascinating facts – named after Little Orphan Annie; Ripple's mentor; victim of a hit-and-run accident; previous owners did not take her to a veterinarian to repair her hip and did not want her anymore; became attached to Mama and used to hobble after her down their small town streets whenever Mama went for a walk until Grandma and Grandpa adopted her and ended her days of wandering; afraid of candle light, jack-o'-lanterns, and thunder; gained her strength and lost her limp as a result of proper care and good nutrition; due to receiving generous portions of love, found her courage and eventually ran the household with a feisty attitude

Choco (aka Choco-Belle):
artistic attributes - reddish-brown Golden Retriever mix
lineage links - non-blood sibling to Frannie and Scappy; belongs with Straw
fascinating facts - faithful; mind of her own; stubborn; generous with kisses; stingy when stealing treats and toys from Frannie

Commander (aka Mander, The Monz):

artistic attributes - white with brown patches and black and brown ticking; large, powerful mix

lineage links - our non-blood canine cousin; belongs with Uncle Randy, Aunt Melissa, Aaron, and Sierra

fascinating facts – named after Commander Cody and His Lost Planet Airmen; known for his domineering personality and strong, definitive character

Frannie (aka Francenia Lucia, Frannie Lu, Francini Houdini):

artistic attributes - Australian Cattle Dog or Heeler with red ticking; breathtakingly beautiful

lineage links - non-blood sibling of Choco and Scappy; belongs with Straw; named after Grandpa's Aunt Fran

fascinating facts - escape artist extraordinaire; found roaming the busy streets of Austin by herself; has survived crossing four lanes of traffic at five o'clock, accidental ingestion of rat poison, and being hit by a car while making an escape from her fenced yard; always ready for fun; likes to bark about it!!!

Frisky George (aka Dr. George):

artistic attributes - handsome brown and black dog with a soft, wavy coat; nicely scented paws

lineage links - belongs with Grandma and Grandpa; grew up with Mama and her siblings

fascinating facts - perfect family dog; gentle; clever; birthday reveler; excellent bedside manner; ham for picture posing; master thief

Scappy (aka Scappy-D):

artistic attributes - all black Heeler cross with a short, stocky body that moves like a sausage-shaped tank

lineage links - non-blood sibling of Choco and blood-donor sibling of Frannie; belongs with Straw; son of a feisty, faithful Blue Heeler named Dottie

fascinating facts - smart; minds well and goes with the flow; faithful protector; sturdy; opened his home to Choco and Frannie

Tasha (aka Tashita):

artistic attributes -golden brown, stocky mix

lineage links - non-blood sibling of fluffy Buffy; belongs with our treasured adopted family, fun-loving Uncle Steve and Aunt Marilyn

fascinating facts - dubbed "the Golden Girls" along with Jessie; part of the Thanksgiving Day group diners; intense dislike of cats in younger years, mellowed and became more receptive to feline friends in later years

T.C.:

artistic attributes - light brown and blonde Pekinese

lineage links - our best friend; belongs with David, who is our neighbor, godfather, and adopted uncle

fascinating facts - amazingly smart; feisty; likes to go on walks with us around the neighborhood; petite appetite; highly sociable

Kit-Kat Club Connections (Feline Friends)

Captain Kitty (aka CK):

artistic attributes - silver tabby; big-boned; hefty; soft to the touch

lineage links - hobo who landed on Straw's doorstep

fascinating facts - totally mellow toward people; dislikes other cats; supervises work projects in yard; has Straw wrapped around his little paw; ultimate cool cat; loaded with cattitude

Cato (aka Cates):

artistic attributes - seal point Himalayan; dashingly handsome

lineage links - belongs with Auntie Carol and Uncle Charlie; Ketra's non-blood sibling; our feline cousin

fascinating facts – sick stray who was deposited at the animal clinic and shortly after adopted by Auntie Carol (a case of love at first sight); has a purrfectly pleasant personality; sociable; a friend to all

Country Kitty (aka KK, Katrina):

artistic attributes - absolutely beautiful tortoiseshell with a distinctive orange patch on the left side of her face

lineage links - our feline sibling

fascinating facts - discovered in the remote country by Auntie Carol; when first found, had a long wound on her abdomen that required stitches; tiny package of pure force; terrorist to other cats; known for tormenting Mattie; surveyor of her kingdom from the rooftop; athletic busy-ball champion; kindred spirit with Rattles, a KK look-and-act-alike cat (yet another neighboring cat who enjoys lounging and eating on Mama's front porch)

Decker (aka Pooty, Poo, D-Man, Stinky, Tinks, Beefy Boy, Pud, C. K. Dexter Haven, Decker McMan McMoogal Me, Poobert, Catman, Mills Lane):

artistic attributes - classic stealth black cat; sleek coat as dark as night; pure pink pads; solid frame; top of head smells sweet

lineage links - our feline sibling

fascinating facts - stray that Mama found abandoned at Decker Lake; renown for his feisty attitude and bully-boy tactics toward other cats; bursting with cattitude; madcap and mischievous to the max; high-pitched meow; yanks hair with his teeth to wake you up; supervisor of work projects of any nature; shopping bag investigator; fun-loving; the paw is quicker than the eye when playing; bathroom monitor; dirt roller; makes mincemeat of wicker furniture; expert at emptying Christmas bags filled with catnip toys; listens and responds to Grandma's phone messages to him; likes to have his chin rubbed; enjoys a peaceful snooze on a kitty cat catnip mat; naps well with others; expert at cuddling; sweet baby boy; content biscuit maker (kneads paws with total pleasure); nosy neighbor; rallies from compromised health; the Comeback Cat; has lived nine lives and then some; known and loved by the entire neighborhood

Jonnie Reb:

artistic attributes - silver-gray tabby; budding beauty

lineage links - member of a tribe of neighborhood cats (Licorice, Poof Muffin, and Cupcake) that began to assemble on Mama's doorstep for chow; living paw-to-mouth on handouts until she captured Mama's heart and home

fascinating facts - sweet, timid girl trying to find her place in the world

Ketra (aka Boogie, Boogie Two Shoes, Sugar Booger, Kee Kee, Keats, Babs):
artistic attributes - gorgeous, long-haired, pure-white princess
lineage links - belongs with Auntie Carol and Uncle Charlie; Cato's non-blood sibling; our feline cousin
fascinating facts – juvenile barn cat rescued by Aunt Nova and adopted by Auntie Carol; known to participate in some friendly rough-housing with Jessie; shy in early years, but found her voice in later years; adored by her family

Licorice (aka Licor, Liquor):
artistic attributes - sturdy gray cat
lineage links - biological brother of Cupcake and Poof Muffin (other members of Jonnie Reb's tribe); neighborhood cat who, after frequenting the homes of Susan, George, Isabelle, Don, Katie, and Angie for food and attention, eventually adopted Mama
fascinating facts - deaf; street-wise; sweet; gentle

Mattie Lou (aka Lou, Mattie Lucini Weini Chili McBeanie, Mattsie, Luscious Lou, Loubert, Matilda, Little Mattie Lou Who, Lula Belle, The Queen, Matina):
artistic attributes - long-haired brown tabby with tweaks of orange; deep green eyes; bobcat-style ears with tufts of hair; long, curved whiskers; ballerina-posed front paws with orange tips; classic pretty kitty
lineage links - our feline sibling
fascinating facts - deserted at the animal clinic where Mama worked; had extensive work on a shattered right hind leg that was slow to heal; proverbial scaredy-cat in her younger days, queen of all she surveys in her older days; catnip-crazed cat; geisha-girl eyes; a hank of hair and a piece of bone; tiny mini-package of pure daintiness; could be blown over by a gentle breeze; pleasing purr box;

strong set of lungs for decibel-breaking yowling in geriatric years; She Who Never Sleeps Except When Mama Is Gone (serenades with meows and yowls all through the night); Decker's Little Big Sister; favorite collar dons a stylish green plaid bow

Mr. Black (aka Mr. Blackfoot):
artistic attributes - only marking that strayed from his name was a white "V" on his belly
lineage links - our feline sibling
fascinating facts - wild-and-crazy cat who moved into our yard; captured in live trap by Mama; nervous cat who was tamed; dubbed "Mr. Blackfoot" due to staying so close to Mama that he was always under her feet; one of Jessie's favorite playmates; feisty, yet gentle

Otis (aka Otis McBotis, Skinny Man, Skinny Mon):
artistic attributes - tall, large-boned, gray tabby
lineage links - stray who adopted Mama and the clinic folks
fascinating facts – found doing the stray cat strut; named after Otis Campbell on *The Andy Griffith Show* because he checked himself into a cage at the clinic every day for three hots and a cot; witty kitty; Decker's nemesis; target of the wrath of irate mockingbirds

Sylvia (aka Syb-a-dee, Sybbie, Syb, Sybson, Tibbs, Angelface):
artistic attributes - coat soft as a rabbit's; pure white with patches of gray tabby, including a series of five "widow's peaks" of gray tabby on her forehead
lineage links - our feline sibling
fascinating facts - found on a neighbor's porch with a bleeding wound on her cheek due to an abscessed upper premolar; known for being a feisty fighter with our other feline siblings and for taking up periodic residence on our roof; mighty huntress; One Courageous Cat; chronic dental problems with few teeth remaining (but still never missed a meal of dry or canned food!); impressive purr box; dedicated biscuit maker

Tater (aka Tater-Bug, Tater-Boy, Tater Tuna, The Gentle Giant, King of the Cats):

artistic attributes - broad brown tabby with large, soft paws (big raccoon kitty paws); always has the look of surprise on his face; top of head smells earthy

lineage links - our feline sibling

fascinating facts - left at the veterinary clinic where Mama worked because his owner could no longer cope with his chronic urinary blockages; never had a urinary blockage after moving in with us (a good diet goes a long way); the original Captain Kitty; unlike many cats, recognizes and responds to his name; always enjoys a good catnip bag; squish kitty (lowers his body just out of reach when somebody tries to pet him); bathroom monitor; first cat to ever own Mama; kind with a gentle nature and wise ways; a friend to all dogs, cats, and people; reason Mama started to adopt additional cats

People Pals

Anne:

puppy pal partner - our adopted aunt; belongs to Shanghai (a gruff and grumpy, but lovable, Keeshond), Amber (a medium-sized, liver-colored, amiable girl whose nose Jessie likes to nip), and Augusta (a large, white with black mix possessing a powerful personality), plus other critters too numerous to name

friendly features - works at the animal clinic; a very close friend of Mama's; has an animal-compassionate mom, Simone; strong with a soft heart; has the reputation for giving a people pal the shirt off her back and going to any measures to provide care and comfort to a critter

Bob:

puppy pal partner - our adopted uncle

friendly features - best friend to our doctor, David; known for taking us on many wondrous outings and road trips and for understanding what it means to belong to a puppy pal

Auntie Carol:

puppy pal partner - has the privilege of being the aunt of two perfect, precocious, precious puppy pals (us, of course!)

friendly features - Mama's sister; the best aunt a puppy pal could ever have; known for taking us on fun-filled excursions and providing us with fantastic treats and care packages; other claim to fame is belonging to sleek Stella Blue, Ketra, and Cato, our feline cousins; along with Uncle Charlie adopted two additional stray cats, cute Kasha and sinewy Simba

David:

puppy pal partner - our adopted uncle (with a black beard) and godfather; belongs to our best friend, T.C.

friendly features - neighbor who lives in a garage apartment across the street from us; one of our sitters when Mama's away; known for going on late afternoon walks with us and co-hosting puppy pal parties laden with delectable treats; treasured friend; one of our very favorite people pals

David:

puppy pal partner - our adopted uncle (with a red beard); belongs to a swift-paced set of sight hounds (such as Salukis, Borzois, and Greyhounds)

friendly features - our kindhearted doctor with whom Mama worked for 14 years; a very special friend and caregiver to all of us; generous in every aspect of his life

Diana:

puppy pal partner - our adopted aunt

friendly features - along with husband, Robert, Sarah, and Travis, provided a fine home to a cluster of cats, a bevy of birds, and a force of fish; one of our sitters when Mama's away; always there for us with a helping hand, a kind word, pats on the back, and hugs

Grandma:

puppy pal partner - belongs to our family predecessors and mentors, Frisky and Annie

friendly features - Mama's mama; the truly impeccable picture of grandmotherly perfection; known for sending us cards, treats, and care packages and for understanding what we mean to Mama

Grandpa:

puppy pal partner - belongs to our family predecessors and mentors, Frisky and Annie

friendly features - Mama's father; Grandpa (with a capital "G") lovingly says it all; along with Grandma, helped teach Mama how to respect all living creatures; fun-loving; immediate connection with and loved by all puppy pals; idolized by Ripple

Uncle Jeff:

puppy pal partner - our uncle; belongs to Tanner, an impressive white force to encounter, and a whole team of other sled dogs who are our Canadian canine cousins

friendly features - Mama's brother; known for taking us on outdoor adventures, including hiking, rock climbing, canoeing, and camping; really knows how to interact with puppy pals on a one-on-one basis; adored by us; Aunt Jill and their tenderhearted kids, Jeremy and Juli, help him care for his pack of pups

Joyce:

puppy pal partner - our adopted aunt; belongs to numerous critters including Jade (a good-natured, lean, gray Greyhound), Elsie (a charming Whippet with a cow pattern of light brown on white), Zola (a fast-track Whippet complete with racing stripes on her coat), and Caira (a tan Greyhound with a sweet disposition)

friendly features - our caring doctor with whom Mama worked for 14 years; one of Mama's best friends; raised her child, Gene, to become a rescuer and defender of critters; there for everyone at all times; always willing to help, support, and comfort

319

Liz:

puppy pal partner - our adopted aunt; belongs to Esther and her daughter, Pearl, two petite, enchanting Whippets

friendly features - worked at the animal clinic; known for giving us tender loving care; along with husband, Robbie, always lets critters run the home; understands how difficult it is to lose a special being

Mama:

puppy pal partner - belongs to us and our own personal kit-kat club

friendly features - we share our home and our hearts; there's nothing we won't do for each other; shared tales with us from 14 years of working at an animal clinic; fondly nicknamed "Mama" because she protects us, provides us with family, friends, food, and fun, and offers a home filled with unlimited unconditional love

Mary:

puppy pal partner - our adopted aunt; belongs to Shea (a large, white German Shepherd loaded with personality) and J. Frank (a sturdily built, black and brown mix with a calm, patient disposition)

friendly features - worked for a short while at the animal clinic with Mama; a good friend to us all; known for supporting Mama and us through health problems or other tough times; featured Ripple in her photo gallery display, *Unusual Pets and Their People* (see cover photo)

Nova:

puppy pal partner - our adopted aunt; belongs to the mighty, yet gentle, Ezra and a fluffy Keeshond named Beau

friendly features - along with kids, Zachary and Alysia, cares for a myriad of critters; close friends with Uncle Vern and with Marsha, a true friend to all animals; understands the deep grief associated with losing a pet; supportive of Mama and us through times of crisis

Uncle Randy:

puppy pal partner - our uncle; belongs to Commander and Abbey

friendly features - Mama's brother; known for teasing Ripple, who savors the fun they have had together through the years; shared his home with Ripple and Mama when they first moved to Austin; likes to go on spur-of-the-moment outings to various parks; along with Aunt Melissa raised two critter-loving children, Aaron and Sierra

Shannon:

puppy pal partner - our adopted aunt; belongs to Rose (a lovely yellow Labrador mix) and Sophie (a black and brown, mid-sized sweetheart of a dog)

friendly features - worked at the animal clinic for several years with Mama; known for being one of the kindest and most persevering puppy-loving souls we have ever met; along with husband, Joe, has rescued many forlorn puppy pals and provided them with an exceptionally loving home; avid supporter of Animal Trustees of Austin

Straw:

puppy pal partner - belongs to Scappy, Choco, and Frannie

friendly features - longtime friend of ours and Mama's; known for caring about his puppy pals and having some exciting life adventures with them; arranges his home for the comfort of his puppy pals; also belongs to Captain Kitty

Susan:

puppy pal partner - our adopted aunt

friendly features - one of Mama's best friends; known for demonstrating that she genuinely cares about us and innately knows how much our mama cherishes us; understands the grieving process and gently supports you through it; she and Uncle Gary belong to Josh and Junior, two kit-kats that Jessie has enjoyed tormenting through the years; raised two cat-caring kids, Jon and Beth

About The Author

Ripple and Jessie have spent their lives with the person who belongs to them, Pamela Wilson. Ms. Wilson has received awards such as Humane Educator, Veterinary Technician of the Year, and Alumni Achievement. Although she is not a veterinarian, she worked at an animal clinic for numerous years. She currently works with zoonoses at a state health department; additionally, she teaches veterinary medical terminology. She earned a BS in zoology and a MEd in health education, plus she is a Registered Veterinary Technician and a Certified Health Education Specialist. The wise teachings of fictional furry friends are in her children's book, *Tales From Tubblewood: A Duck For All Seasons*.

Printed in the United States
144454LV00003BA/6/A